Ulster

A Case Study in Conflict Theory

Ulster

A Case Study in Conflict Theory

R. S. P. Elliot
and John Hickie

Longman

Longman Group Limited
London
Associated companies, branches and representatives
throughout the world

First published 1971

ISBN 0 582 11385 7

Printed in Great Britain by
The Camelot Press Ltd. London and Southampton

To Lesley and Margot

Contents

Acknowledgements

We would like to thank Ann Reid and Jane Taylor who came on the original data collection exercises and Joan Peake, Carol Williams, Lindsay Barker, Wendy Freston, Jennifer Barnett, and Lorna Hamilton, who at various stages typed parts of the manuscript.

Our thanks also go to our colleagues at the Conflict Research Unit, the Centre for the Analysis of Conflict, Richardson Institute for Conflict and Peace Research and the Institute for Peace and Conflict Research, and to Vladimar Peksa who helped with the computerisation of the results. Finally we wish to thank the political leaders in Ulster and Eire who spared the time to talk to us.

Preface

This book describes one of the first attempts in the comparatively new discipline of conflict research to analyse an ongoing conflict situation through standardised interviews with leaders of all the interested parties.

This project was financed out of a one-year grant of £7,447 from the Social Science Research Council, given originally to the Conflict Research Unit for the purpose of exploring decision making under stress in laboratory conditions. In order to balance the laboratory approach we felt it necessary to study decision making in live situations. One of the real situations the Unit analysed was local government council meetings. However, the Unit was primarily concerned with decision making in crises and ultimately hoped to have findings which were applicable to decision makers in international crisis situations. At this stage we were already in the process of planning a study of foreign ministries for which we subsequently received a small grant from the SSRC. It was felt that a study of decision makers in the political arena would complement the proposed study. This was one reason for our interest in Ulster.

Also, one of the authors (John Hickie) had recently completed field research in Cyprus, which like Ulster was an intercommunal conflict area where each of the opposing sides had links with outside governments. The second reason therefore was to see whether insights gained in Cyprus were applicable to Ulster.

Thirdly, there was a continuing need for empirical data to test theoretical assumptions. The literature on international relations, conflict research, and social psychology abounds with competing theories about the way the world functions. One of the reasons for this plethora is simply that there is little available data against which hypotheses can be falsified.

A final reason was that by definition the Unit was interested in conflict and the situation in Ulster provided an opportunity to develop both methodological techniques and greater understanding of the dynamics of conflict. In addition, Ulster had a number of advantages in that it was close at hand and could thus be studied without transgressing beyond the scarce resources in terms of finance and personnel that the project possessed.

Therefore the Ulster project complemented the laboratory work by enabling one to see whether conclusions arrived at under experimental conditions would prove correct in a real life situation.

The outline of the book reflects the fact that whereas as we intended this project to be a study of Ulster we found that this became a subsidiary interest to the practical, methodological and theoretical problems which the research raised. The book starts with a chapter introducing the theoretical aspects of conflict theory before moving on in Chapter 2 to a brief historical account of the Ulster situation. Chapter 3 attempts to relate conflict theory to intercommunal conflict. Chapters 4 and 5 outline the problems of administration, method and theory involved in the data collection while Chapter 6 discusses the results. Chapter 7 considers the theoretical and value implications of the research. Any reader interested specifically in a description of the Ulster conflict should concentrate on Chapters 2 and 6.

Introduction

The history of British conflict research

An account of British conflict research necessarily begins with a brief history of the discipline, which is a sure key to understanding its major purposes and goals.

The first major English institution to carry out specific academic research into the causes of peace and conflict was the Peace Knowledge Foundation which set up a Peace Knowledge Centre in Lancaster in the early sixties. This Centre was a private organisation, financed by private funds. A number of its seminars were attended by some postgraduate students from the Sociology and Operations Research Departments of Lancaster University. The core of this group consisted of Robin Jenkins, John Macrae and Paul Smoker. The group produced a roneoed newsletter, circulated to several universities, in which they reported seminar discussions, reviewed books and commented on world news. At that time they were what could be best described as an action-oriented interest group. Their dominant perspectives were sociological, and they were generally more radical than any of the others becoming interested in the area. From the beginning the Lancaster group wished to affect the world; theirs was not a discipline which existed only in the academic journals.

In so far as this group began to establish a discipline of peace research designed to grapple with the causes of conflict at many social levels, they should be counted as pioneers. They were, however, only an informal group; there were no salaries, no positions. In fact, it was to be some years before the necessary money was donated to research of this kind.

In the early 1960s there was no coordinated effort in this field in London except for a small group of academics gathered round Jack Mongar, Cedric Smith and Lionel Penrose; the first a Professor of Pharmacology and the latter two Professors of Genetics at University College, London. They held seminars and discussions on some aspects of aggression in man. In their aims the

London group, and particularly Professor Mongar, differed from the group in Lancaster. Whereas the Northerners were more concerned with the need for political action, Professor Mongar was concerned with the need to instigate behaviourally oriented studies on conflict in a university framework.

This was to prove a difficult task. The social science departments were already short of funds and space. Furthermore, the few who had heard of peace research regarded it as something of a Trojan horse; it borrowed its concept freely from all the social sciences, adapting each of them as it went and it might well have looked threatening to the sociologists.

There was the additional problem that there was no substantial body of scholarly writing on the subject in this country. In the 1930s the mathematician Lewis Fry Richardson[1] had collected a large amount of material on human fighting at the international level and had described the construction of a mathematical model for plotting and predicting the rise and fall of international tension. However, his brilliant work had long since been forgotten. It was only reintroduced to the British in the 1960s by American scholars.

At this stage it proved impossible to follow the lead of the United States. There, the growth point for conflict studies had been the discipline of international relations which, in the previous decade, had changed from a historical/legal course in current affairs to a behavioural study of international interactions. The prestigious *Journal of Conflict Resolution*, edited and published by a group of international relations scholars, stimulated the co-ordination of research into the causes of conflict by other academic disciplines. Unfortunately, in Great Britain a similar revolution had not taken place; it is, in fact, happening only just now. A historical arts discipline would hardly provide the organisational base for yet another upstart social science. This peace research was the concern solely of the group of postgraduates in Lancaster and a handful of professors in London with no substantial literature to its credit save for two forgotten books published twenty years previously.

In London, the CIBA Foundation had been established after the war to 'further interest and cooperation in research bearing on human health, medicine and biology'; up to late 1962 it had been concerned exclusively with the physical sciences. Its then Deputy Director, the physicist Dr A. V. S. de Reuck, felt that for CIBA the time had come to encourage humanitarian research in the social sciences in such areas as race relations, drug addiction and mental subnormality. Professor Mongar who was collaborating with Dr de Reuck on a book on drug addiction interested him in peace research and introduced him to Professors Smith and Penrose. De Reuck decided that it was an area appropriate for CIBA activities.

Mongar, de Reuck and Smith planned a three-forked approach to the problem. They called a conference on conflict research in Windsor in 1963 in order to sound out academic opinion in the country, and to educate the participants in the theoretical assumptions of conflict research. The idea for this conference had already been canvassed with the Lancaster group who were in favour and did much to help organise it.

At the same time a miniature propaganda campaign was organised which concentrated on explaining peace research to persons of some influence in the academic establishment. Later on, these contacts were directly or indirectly, to bear fruit. By 1964, after the Windsor conference, there was a network of people interested in furthering peace research in an academic framework.

Thirdly it was decided to encourage well-known academics to write on peace research, in order to establish the credibility of the subject in Great Britain; thus prospective writers were brought together at a symposium organised under CIBA auspices. They included the then little-known Herbert Marcuse and John Bowlby an expert on behavioural research on learning and imprinting in small children. At the same time Jack Mongar had met Dr John Burton, ex-Director of the Australian Department of External Affairs, who had already written two books on international relations in a behaviourally oriented framework.[2] He came to England at the end of 1964 on a Quaker fellowship and in this country immediately became concerned with the organisation of peace research and international relations, receiving active support from the Quakers. However, the report of the CIBA symposium was not published until the summer of 1965 because few of the contributors could agree on the relevance of each other's contribution. Despite this, the published symposium remains one of the first authoritative works on peace research.[3]

The meeting at Windsor proved a stimulus to the growth of the discipline. Initial difficulties to persuade some of the American experts to attend—they hesitated because they had never heard of any interest in the subject in this country—were eventually overcome and the conference led to two resolutions. The first was to set up conflict research in a university framework; the second was to set up a conflict research society to collect money to finance research fellowships in the universities, to publish a journal, and to establish the discipline professionally.

Meanwhile, the circle of interested academics had widened and a series of seminars was held at University College, London, the London School of Economics and the Tavistock Institute. By this time John Burton was teaching international relations at University College, London. At the London School of Economics two social scientists, Dr Emanuel de Kadt and Dr A. N. Oppenheim, had become interested in the field and were instrumental in arranging seminars. De Kadt later left for South America; Oppenheim retained his interest and was later to become a member of the Conflict Research Society's Council and its Honorary Secretary.

Some seminars on conflict research were also run by Victor Brix, who led a social cybernetics group[4] at University College. So by the end of 1964 the discipline was beginning to emerge. At a meeting at the London School of Economics the constitution of the Conflict Research Society was drawn up. Cedric Smith was the first Chairman and John Burton the first Honorary Secretary.

The lead was then taken up by John Burton. His intention was to get done some active research work that could be immediately applied to international conflict. He wanted to set up a sort of social scientists' Pugwash; Pugwash is an international society composed of physical scientists who are concerned about the misuses and applications of their work, particularly in the nuclear field—an apolitical body which meets occasionally in different parts of the world and discusses arms control and allied subjects. The Chairman of Pugwash was then John Rotblatt, Professor of Physics at St Bartholomew's Hospital, who, however, maintained that the point of Pugwash was that it was apolitical. He felt a social scientists' Pugwash, concerned with the making of policy pronouncements, would be nothing *but* political. Burton therefore chose a different name for the group and convened a trial international meeting of Coriopas[5] near Paris, composed of academics and politicians from all over the world. Apparently his intention was to set up a type of foreign office without a state, an organisation of academics who could participate in world affairs. The Quakers already had such an organisation, but it was not academically supported.

The participants at these meetings finally split into three distinct groups. The first group claimed that any new pressure group would be of little use since there was quite enough politicking already. The second group felt that in the present, rudimentary state of knowledge prescription and recommendation would be wrong. What was required was an international institution devoted to pure research in order to make prescription possible at some later date. The third group, led by John Burton, maintained that enough was known about the etiology of human conflict to allow for a body of academics to make action-oriented statements. In the event, nothing came out of the meeting. Undismayed, John Burton asked the CIBA Foundation to arrange a meeting of academics in the United Kingdom to discuss the situation.

Meanwhile, the state of conflict research in Great Britain had considerably improved. Nineteen sixty-five was a significant year : Lancaster University decided to institute a peace research fellowship in the operations research department which went to Dr Michael Nicholson, a mathematical economist, previously at Cambridge University, the Massachussets Institute of Technology and the Oslo Peace Research Institute. In 1965 the group centred around the Peace Knowledge Centre at Lancaster was able to institute a full-time Peace Research Centre with grants from Cadbury and Nuffield. It started to carry out active research which even at this date, seemed to attract little attention in London. By this time the Conflict Research Society was well established. The CIBA discussion meeting was arranged in early 1965. It went on for two days and roughly the same division of opinion emerged as at the abortive Coriopas meeting; those wanting a purely research oriented international institution won the day. It was resolved to establish an International Peace Research Association which would carry out work of the same order as the Conflict Research Society, but on an international level, financed by subscriptions from national members. The first conference was held in Groningen in the summer of 1965, and since then nine international meetings have been held, allowing for free exchange of information throughout the world. The Lancaster group was thereafter closely involved in the activities of IPRA.

There was as yet no research institute in London. During the seminars held for the purposes of writing the book *Conflict in Society*, John Burton again had suggested that enough was known about the nature of conflict to carry out some sort of action research in the international system. Letters were accordingly written to the representatives of two states then engaged in armed conflict, inviting them to a research meeting in London. The invitations were on Tavistock notepaper and the meetings were held at the CIBA Foundation. Continuous meetings between the diplomats of the two states (who normally would not come into contact) and a panel of social scientists were held for a week, and thereafter intermittently for a period of six months until early 1966. The results were encouraging; out of these meetings came the

B

first major theoretical concepts of the technique later known as 'controlled communication'.[6]

Secondly, and much more important, the results were impressive enough to persuade both Lord Evans, Provost of University College, London, and the Social Science Research Council, that a centre should be set up to develop this technique of interstate mediation. Thus in 1966 the Centre for the Analysis of Conflict was set up at University College, London, under the Directorship of John Burton. Michael Nicholson from Lancaster and A. V. S. de Reuck from the CIBA Foundation joined the team there as did C. R. Mitchell, Michael Banks, both international relations theorists, and Frank Edmead, an expert on South-East Asia from *The Guardian*. They later held a series of controlled communications, the results of which have been published.[5] This Centre was, however, heavily oriented towards international relations and to the exploitation of one particular technique. At the beginning of 1967 the Conflict Research Unit, under the directorship of A. N. Oppenheim, was set up at LSE to study conflict research at all social levels.

The picture was nearly complete. The final move came when it was decided to amalgamate the London Conflict Research Society and the Peace Research Centre in Lancaster. The PRC was moving to London, anyway, and it was decided that it should become the research arm of the CRS. The CRS and IPRA meetings had always done much to bring the two groups together. The PRC (now known as the Richardson Institute) in London was officially inaugurated on 7 February 1970. Once again its areas of research were wide, ranging from a study of South African imperialism to the development of new methods of data handling in the social sciences. The disciplines of its employees were wide and varied, from political sciences and sociology to mathematics and engineering.

This is the present state of the discipline; it is therefore appropriate that we now shift our attention to the area of theoretical concern. What is conflict research? What does it study?

[1] L. F. Richardson, *Arms and Insecurity*, Stevens, 1960.

[2] See J. W. Burton, *The Alternative,* Sydney, Morgans Publications; and *Peace Theory: Preconditions of disarmament*, New York, Knopf, 1962.

[3] *Conflict and Society*, ed. De Reuck and Knight, Churchill, 1965.

[4] Social Cybernetics Group, *A Cybernetic Approach to Conflict*, London, Conflict Research Society, 1966 (mimeographed).

[5] Committee for Research on International Peace and Security.

[6] J. W. Burton, *Conflict and Communication: the use of controlled communication in international relations*, Macmillan, 1969.

Conflict theory and methods in Great Britain

Peace research is first and foremost an eclectic body of knowledge, freely borrowing its concepts and techniques from other disciplines. In consequence it is inaccurate to talk of 'conflict theory', if by the word 'theory', one means a system of logically interrelated and empirically tested rules and principles. It is in reality a mixture of *hunch* and theorising, sometimes illuminated by research findings, more often not.

The intention in this chapter is to present conflict research in a reasonably orderly fashion, so that at least its broad outlines may be discerned. The danger of such a procedure is that by trying to introduce clarity the authors will impose a unity which does not exist. The alternative of describing chaos in a chaotic fashion is no less attractive.

Any discussion of this nature must start with definitions, the most important being the definition of conflict. Even here there is disagreement, but many writers on the subject would at least agree that the term refers to some form of incompatibility between the courses of action open to two or more parties. Thus two buyers may desire the same article, or two governments want the same territory. Such a definition of conflict has the virtue (at least at first sight) of being *objective*. One only has to determine the nature of the goals of any two parties, and estimate the extent to which the realisation of one party's goals frustrates the other in order to determine whether or not there is a conflict.

Even such a simple definition allows us to make some useful distinctions. It is, for example, a logical corollary of this definition of conflict that two parties might not realise they are in conflict. In such cases, one may refer to a *latent* as opposed to a *manifest* conflict situation, since the latter only exists when the parties subjectively perceive themselves to be in conflict. The formulation of such definitions is an important part of the creation of a new discipline because it provides a vocabulary and allows analytic

problems to be categorised. For example, it is of central concern to discover under what conditions conflicts remain latent or become manifest to the parties involved. One may go on usefully inspecting the implications of such primary distinctions. For example, we can now see that the two parties may think they are in conflict with each other when in fact there is no real incompatibility of interests or goals. Robin Jenkins has applied this distinction in arguing that the religious conflict in Ulster is an *unreal* conflict; that is, allegiance to one religion does not logically imply hostility towards members of other religious groups in the same society. Such a distinction is more than mere polemic because it invites an enquiry into the nature of the real conflict. Jenkins's answer is that the real conflict is between rich and poor; since this is not perceived the consequent tensions find expression in religious conflict.

This analysis also provides us with an illustration of the eclectic nature of the discipline. Jenkins's argument is based on a social psychological theory to the effect that frustration leads to aggression which if blocked in one direction will manifest itself in another. A chain is thus set up whereby the invention of new distinctions, e.g., between 'real' and 'unreal' conflict, leads to the need to find alternative explanations. This in turn leads to the formulation of new research questions, in this case linking economic factors to religious violence.

The frustration/aggression hypothesis is only one of many borrowed from neighbouring disciplines. However, not only are hypotheses and theories borrowed but also sets of distinctions and definitions similar to those referred to. For example, from psychology and in particular social psychology we gain an awareness that conflicts can take place at different levels of experience. Thus conflicts may derive from the fact that the parties concerned have different values, different goals, or merely different patterns of behaviour. If someone is smoking in a non-smoking compartment merely out of habit, he may happily respond to an objection and extinguish his cigarette. However, we may find that he places a high value on rejecting authority, so that for him the conflict is a matter of deeply held principle. To use a more serious example, attempts to hold on to colonial control led to a grave conflict because of a failure to appreciate the deep values that were at stake for the subject peoples. We are generally aware of such factors in a conflict when we have the advantages of hindsight. One of the advantages of a well formulated analytical framework is that we may derive from it a little foresight.

It is apparent that one may go on to build up a complex set of definitions and distinctions. It is not our purpose to do this here; we merely recommend that the interested reader follow up the references at the end of this chapter. We should, however, point out that it is possible to categorise any conflict along a number of dimensions in a sophisticated fashion allowing for more detailed analysis than is commonly found. Let us make one more distinction before we go further. It can be argued that in Ulster both poor sectors of society lose from the conflict they are waging. They fight in part because they think that any gain by one party can only be a loss to the other, and *vice versa*. To use terminology borrowed in this instance from mathematical game theory, such a relationship would be described as *fixed sum*; if the gains and losses made by both sides are added up the final figure is always the same because the size of the cake is fixed. This is in contrast to a *variable sum* relationship where both parties can positively gain from cooperation, not necessarily at the expense of each other. In this case, a simple distinction takes us into the heart of a major theoretical debate; that is, whether there is in nature such a thing as a fixed sum situation or whether it is merely a matter of perception. Some analysts would maintain that there is never a situation where one side has to lose, merely situations in which one or more of the parties perceives this to be the case.

We are already far from the rudimentary definitions with which we started this chapter and in an area best discussed later in the book. For the present there remain many basic notions about conflict to discuss.

It is important to notice that so far we have said nothing about the behaviour of parties to a conflict. There is a distinction made here between the nature of a conflict, and conflict-related behaviour. Once a conflict has become manifest, the parties must decide, collectively or individually, on how to resolve it, by fighting, talking, retreating, or whatever. A game theorist, Anatole Rapaport, has made several distinctions between types of conflict behaviour.[1] Each has a different background, pattern of development and distribution of predictable outcomes.

In a *fight* type of conflict the self-control and mutual control of the actors decline rapidly, the reactions of each actor serving as starting points for similar counteractions by the other. These processes tend to be automatic and mindless, as with novice draughts players whose inept moves seem to have been obvious and necessary. Thus it is that statesmen find they have no alternative but to make moves which only exacerbate the situation.

Game conflicts are situations in which each player maintains rational control over his own moves, though not necessarily over their outcome. Often he will not know completely what his opponent can do, or may plan or decide to do. Faced with such uncertainty, each player must plan his moves on the most rational guess he can make. This is an area where formal strategic analysis is particularly relevant.

Lastly, conflicts in which the adversaries are changing each others motives, values or cognitive images of reality may be called *debates* in the strict sense of the term. This should not be confused with what we normally think of as a debate, that is, a situation where two parties have no intention of changing their position but only of impressing a third party such as a magistrate or a judge. True, dialogue in which the parties are able to change each other's motives lies at the heart of conflict resolution. Because the book is concerned chiefly with this area, we will say no more about it here, save to point out that the ability to change another party's mind can be just as likely a force for the worse as for the better.

We have, therefore, three different categorisations, all of which refer to very different social phenomena and which, of course, can again go deeper. Once the level or realm of any particular conflict behaviour has been identified in this way the mechanics of it have to be inspected. For example, what happens to small groups, organisations or communities when they are put under stress in conflict? Here again there is a rich area of study which, of necessity, has to draw on a wide range of social theory. For example, L. F. Richardson[2] and, more recently, M. B. Nicholson[3] have demonstrated that some fight situations such as escalating arms races can be described in mathematical terms. Richardson postulates an arms race model where each party bases its arms acquisitions on an estimate of its own and the other party's strength plus a 10 per cent safety margin. It is easy to see that should two parties adopt such a formula the situation will rapidly deteriorate into a race towards destruction. Richardson pointed out that such races can be plotted with the use of linear differential equations. This is probably a trite example of conflict mechanics, but should serve to demonstrate the nature of the study as well as indicating its potential complexity.

THE PARTIES TO A CONFLICT[4]

We also have to pay attention to the actors involved in any conflict. Different sizes and types of actor will obviously react in different ways. In the normal course of events most of the simple labels we apply to parties in conflict are hopelessly inadequate. For example, when we say that 'a nation is at war' we mean that a particular social aggregate, labelled 'a nation' but in fact a collection of classes, government, interest groups and organisations, is faced with a certain situation that all will probably perceive as a conflict in different ways and accordingly react differently towards it. Their orientations will be consistently mediated by their interactions within the nations and with their opponents.

It is, therefore, fundamental to realise the dynamic aspect of conflict, not only because of the number of different interactions between fixed parties to be watched, but also because the different groupings involved may not remain constant over time. An example is the shifting support for Ian Paisley in Ulster over the last few years.

Leaving that complication aside, there is always the initial problem of defining the units in any conflict. J. W. Burton[5] argues that the bulk of the analysis of conflict in international relations has been misdirected because 'nations' are not real units—they are only labels donated by consensus. He maintains that this is true of most social levels and that only by using systems theory can we come to any awareness of who does what, when and where. We shall be inspecting this particular problem later in this chapter, and it is an issue that will occupy us throughout the book.

LEVELS OF CONFLICT

Lastly, in most situations defined as single conflicts there are many different conflicts involved. For example, in an industrial strike situation there may well be conflict within the local union, between the union and the national branch, between the unions and the management, within the management and so forth.[6] In practical terms the first effect of finding so many conflicts is that the analyst usually has to redefine the parties to the conflicts. Even when that has been done there are still problems to be solved, such as, Which is the key conflict? Will resolution of one of the sub-conflicts cause more trouble at another level? And so on.

While one is attempting to resolve such problems all these factors will be shifting and quite probably new conflicts will be replacing or adding to the old ones. It is a matter of common observation that with the development of conflicts original causes and grievances are often forgotten.

All this should be sufficient to suggest that not only do peace researchers differ in their theoretical background and orientations, but that they apply this to an area that is, even in principle, of infinite complexity. Before we can see how researchers tackle these problems we should seek more clarity by looking at the reverse side of the coin.

PEACE

According to Galtung[7] 'peace research is research on the maximisation of peaceful relations between behaviourally defined human groups'. Such a definition, however, is deceptively simple. Let us try to set out a few of the complications. In July 1969 there took place in Paris an 'Advisory Meeting of the Experts on Unesco's Role In Developing Research on Peace Problems'— whose final report contained some comments germane to our present investigation: 'Individual peace researchers define their task as one of accommodating social change in a non-violent way, and to this end they seek to improve the present system, or appropriately to transform it.' The first obvious implication is that peace can only be seen as a function of the structure and processes of political and social systems. Thus peace becomes a property of the whole social order rather than a mere unrelated pathology. The job of the peace researcher will therefore involve a concern with social change and social engineering.

The problem of designing peaceful societies is further complicated by the fact that not all conflict as such is harmful. As the report put it: 'Peace researchers' concern is not to abolish social tensions as such but to distinguish their positive and negative consequences and to facilitate the use of positive aspects of conflict between human groups at all levels.' It may be trite to point out that this is a tall order, but it would certainly not be an understatement; in operational terms such a prescription is not clear. For example, theories of economic development depend on the notion of advancement of the whole society through competition and conflict between its different component groups. Such thinking lies at the root of *laissez-faire* economics. However, acceptance of such a theory depends largely upon one's social class. (This is just one illustration of the many ways in which the values held by the analyst must inevitably creep into thinking about peace.) Nevertheless few would deny the proposition that peace is a process involving an optimum amount of conflict. In fact, in the theories of Coser[8] and Simmel, societies may be regarded as being stitched together by conflicts.

To illustrate this, let us imagine a society with four people in it, A,B,C and D. If for some reason, perhaps wealth, A and B unite against C and D over certain issues, then such theorists would argue that for peace to be maintained within that society, A and C would need some ground to unite against B and D. In this way the conflict gives the society a criss-cross pattern of allegiances and opposition. Conflict is only dysfunctional when all the divisions in the society fall along the same lines. In such a case we speak of a community being *polarised*. Polarisation is defined as a condition where two groups contain all the positive bonds *within* themselves and have only negative bonds *between* themselves.[9]

This leads us to another central problem. In the example we have just given the two groups were hypothetically peaceful within themselves. It is often the case that peaceful at one social level is only gained by conflict at another. A good example of this is South African society, where the agreed life-style of the white community can only be acted out on the basis of conflict against and within the black community. There is a danger here that the decision whether or not a conflict is functional or dysfunctional depends to some extent on the social location of the analyst. The nineteenth-century commentators who spoke of healthy economic competition and postulated Malthusian laws of social evolution were not born into the classes which suffered most from the social order. This is a problem which is central to much of the analysis which we shall present later. We can conclude here with the observation that conflict may simultaneously be functional for some people and dysfunctional for others, and that this involves the values of the analyst to some extent. As the Unesco report says: 'The peace researcher is concerned with all forms of violence; general behavioural violence and hidden structural violence. The structural forms of violence are those institutionalised inequalities within many nations which inhibit social justice and are therefore conducive to behavioural violence. As these structural forms of social injustice exist both at the international and national level, so the peace researcher is led to examine social injustice wherever this is relevant.'

Making peace synonymous with social justice certainly widens our understanding of the word. This widening of the concept has two important practical implications. Firstly the peace researcher must be more firmly embedded in his society than is usually the case with academics. 'He also looks at the groups within a society which contribute to the making of peace; the role of workers, peasants, the middle classes and students and leadership elements in the society. He is further interested in the study of social groupings which generate conflict that sometimes explodes at the international level, such as the activity of guerrilla groups' (Unesco report). Yet at the same time the analyst must maintain some amount of scientific detachment—not an easy task.

The second implication is that peace research has a revolutionary standpoint. As A. J. Muste put it: 'In a world built on violence one must be a revolutionary before one can be a pacifist. The foremost task is to denounce the violence on which the present system is based, and all the suffering—spiritual and material—that this entails for the masses of men throughout the world. . . . So long as we are not dealing honestly and adequately with this 90 per cent of the problem, there is something ludicrous and perhaps hypocritical about our concern over the 10 per cent of physical violence employed by the rebels against oppression.'[10] This means that the concern for peace leads straight into the realm of philosophical social critique, the hereditary domain of the social sciences. (It also means that raising funds for major research projects may encounter obstacles.)

Peace is more than merely the absence of one kind of violence since the command not to fight, from the disinterested pacifist, does not appeal to groups of people who have already decided that it is 'better to die on one's feet than to live on one's knees'. Peace is a function of a total social system and its attainment must therefore involve continuous work. This gives the lie to the simple notion that peace is merely the absence of physical violence. It was in this sense that British colonial administrators talked of bringing peace to the Empire. In order to examine this more closely we must use several more technical terms. We will need to distinguish between conflict *suppression* and conflict *resolution*, and between *negative* peace and *positive* peace.

We can illustrate the first distinction with reference to the conflict in Cyprus. After the bitter intercommunal fighting in 1963, a United Nations peace-keeping force interposed itself between the combatant forces. The fighting stopped but the hostility remained. In fact, because of the lack of communication between the two sides, the hostile stereotypes and misperceptions increased and there now exists a situation of cold war. There is little direct violence between the two communities, but because of the lack of information flowing between them, they consistently surprise and frighten each other so that there is little chance of their basic grudges being resolved.

Opposed to this situation of conflict suppression is that of conflict resolution, where the parties communicate directly with each other and are able to realign their images of the world in accordance with their mutual needs.

In the same way, negative peace is merely a situation of stand-off with a very low level of contact between the parties. In positive peace the two parties actively contribute towards the improvement of their common lot. Every new interaction creates new rewards to both the parties. As we have pointed out, this involves hard work, not least because such cooperation involves substantial costs. As two parties become more dependent upon each other, so they become increasingly vulnerable to each other. They have to expose their weak points, physical and psychological, as when two married people find it increasingly difficult to present their ideal self-image to each other credibly.

It is appropriate to remark here that the fears leaders may feel for the security of their own communities when dropping their defences against other communities are, in their terms of the situation, entirely rational. In the analysis of peace and conflict it is usually apparent that most of the actors in a conflict are carrying out plans that are rational in terms of the situation *as they define it*. Words such as 'irrational' or 'aggressive' are usually devoid of analytical content and mean that their user either misunderstands or distrusts the actions of some party.

This discussion, therefore, finally centres on a consideration of positive peace—that happy condition where the relevant parties are working cooperatively within a common framework and agreed communication patterns, with respect for social justice, producing evenly distributed rewards. As this utopian vision is difficult to discuss in concrete terms, we had better close this particular section by considering just how conflict research works. We will then be in a position to discuss the major contributions to the field.

CONFLICT RESEARCH TECHNIQUES AND APPROACHES

In this section we shall follow closely a set of headings devised by Michael Banks formerly of the Centre for the Analysis of Conflict, which actually delineate the principal types of research done in the field.[11]

Abstract analysis

This refers to the elaboration of conceptual schemes of all kinds.

The extreme instance of this activity is *General Systems Theory*,[12] of which the major derivations, somewhat closer to reality, are structure/functional analysis and communication theory. Briefly, these areas of analysis are concerned with the construction of models of human behaviour and interaction based on the insights into processes of control, communication and pattern maintenance, derived from the study of electronic and biological information systems. (We discuss this area of theory in greater detail later on in the chapter.) The work at this level is extremely abstract, but does provide a framework for any general theory of human conflict and deductive applications from this area have proved fruitful. To quote one analyst: 'Any applied research is an investment for the future. Because we know that human behaviour never repeats itself exactly, it is much more useful to have a general knowledge of present and past phenomena than a detailed knowledge of a particular past event which will only resemble any future event in a very limited sense. The generalising approach may contribute relatively little to the solution of some specific problems, but in the long run it can lead to the solution of a whole class of problems.'

Aspect analysis

By this is meant the kind of study in which it is assumed that the world is too complex to comprehend all at once, either abstractly or in reality. It follows from this that it may be more useful to take a part of a complex problem and to study that part in isolation by focusing attention only on the aspect of real world behaviour which is relevant to the testing of a particular proposition. An example may be a decision-making analysis of a ministry of foreign affairs. The major part of conflict research concerns detailed studies of particular aspects of the world.

Analogue analysis

This may take a variety of forms. What they have in common is the starting proposition that since we know rather more about some social systems than others (e.g. about, say, murder in the family context than about war in the international one), it may be possible to assemble knowledge about higher level social systems by transferring to them any available findings from other analogous systems. For example, the Conflict Research unit has carried out a series of intensive studies of town council meetings. The intention is not to gain knowledge about town councils *per se,* but rather about bargaining processes of conflict resolution not so easily observed elsewhere.

Ethological studies

These are studies of animal behaviour, many aspects of which are obviously analogous to the behaviour of human groups. Territoriality, the development of group norms, the different relationships within and between species, and conflict behaviour, are only the major headings in this area of enquiry. Many readers will be familiar with the works of Desmond Morris, Konrad Lorenz and Robert Ardrey.

The three—abstract analysis, aspect analysis, analogue analysis —headings cover the major area of work carried out on peace research in this country. Mention has been made several times of systems theory both as an integrative theory and as a means of transferring material from one level to another. It is therefore relevant at this point to digress on the nature of such theorising.

SYSTEMS THEORY

(1) Systems analysis

The subject matter under this heading can be divided into two main parts: systems analysis and general systems theory.

A system may be defined as any set of units of the same kind or which interact in some way. Thus a motorcar or an apple or a lake and forest complex may all be defined as systems. Because 'system' is an analytic term, its boundaries are defined by the criteria of exclusion or inclusion laid down by the analyst for the purposes of his research. Thus, for analytic purposes, we may wish to describe the British Prime Minister, the American President and the British Parliament as a system if, for example, we were interested in the special relationship with the U.S.A. In this sense, system is only a way of talking precisely about things. In society, for example, we may talk of the cultural system, concerned with the values, norms and rules of the society; the social system, concerned with different interaction patterns like classes and élites; and the political system, concerned with the authoritative location of values in a society (i.e. who gets what, when and where). It may be objected that system is thus an entirely arbitrary term, and so it is. This is in the nature of all analytic classifications, but those systems which are not relevant to the subject under study will soon be discarded. An example of this is the many redefinitions of atomic systems to be found in physics. The important thing about defining a set of variables as a system is that they should have explanatory or predictive power when tested against reality. Thus, later on in the book, we sometimes define Stormont and Whitehall as one separate interaction system.

Why is this method at all useful or superior to other methods of analysis? Its first advantage is that it gets us away from consensually defined units. There is enormous pressure to interpret events in one way when looking at the world through the mass media and the layman's eye. This may be misleading. For example, in the past the importance of the nation-state unit has been heavily emphasised in the study of international relations. But in Europe, for example, the notion of the nation-state does not explain half of what is going on. We have to think in terms of new systems of interaction if we are to account for events in an increasingly complex world. In Ulster it is useless merely to speak of the Catholic and Protestant communities. The dynamic aspects of the conflict are made up of the interaction of many different subsystems of beliefs, attitudes and behaviour. Until we allow ourselves to take off the public's spectacles we cannot really understand what is going on.

The second advantage of systems analysis is its precise vocabulary. It is not necessary to give it in full here; some examples will suffice.[13] We may distinguish between systems and subsystems, open and closed, stable and unstable systems. Each of these terms has been precisely defined in the literature, so that we have accuracy. Systems analysis is thus to some extent the realisation of the dream of the seventeenth-century rational philosophers that an intellectual language be developed with the precision of mathematics and completely rid of secondary meanings and distortions derived from common usage of the language. Such a vocabulary is vital if we wish to make analogies or homologies between differential social levels. It is no good discussing the extent to which a wildcat strike resembles a guerrilla attack, unless we can define in precisely what respects it is similar and in what respects it is different.

(2) General systems theory

Systems analysis must be distinguished from general systems theory: the latter may be most simply defined as the study of all living systems. It is a theory of open systems that exchange matter and energy with their environment. It copes with complicated concepts such as organisation, teleology, control, self-regulation, differentiation and the like. So far it has found its most spectacular implications in the biological field,[14] yet some others have applied it to political sciences and conflict studies. Deutsch, for example, has described the nation-state as a self-regulating, feedback system.[15] Let us look at a simple behavioural system:

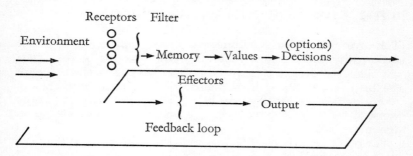

All processing systems (computers, humans and states) are faced with a complex environment which contains much more variety than they can cope with. When this information reaches the system through its receptors (computer inputs, nerves, embassies) it is filtered out, the system seeking only that information which is relevant to its programme. It then compares this information with its memory (data bank, human memory, filing system) to check for familiarity. Once it has combined the new input with any relevant old information it compares it with its values (computer programme, human values, firm's regulations) and, on the basis of this evaluation, it can decide on the relevant range of options that are open. Having decided to take one of these options it effects its decision by implementing one or more of the approaches at its disposal. The output goes into the environment and the results of the output will later be fed back (feed-back loop) into the system, and the whole process will start again.

At this level, machines, people and organisations are similar. The corollary of this is that they will react in similar ways to similar inputs; thus systems may show the effects of being over-loaded or underloaded, pay too much attention to past information or too much to values and so forth. At the present stage of conflict theory most of these ideas are really only heuristic, but the language of general systems theory is used widely in the literature and will tend to crop up in this book. How long it will be before general systems theory is a genuinely predictive tool depends to a large extent upon the amount of field research done. However, even in its present crude state (so far as the social sciences are concerned) it has done much to influence both the major schools of theory which we are about to examine. As is so often the case, it is easiest to describe those schools by referring to the theoretical positions of the two men who lead them.

THE WORK OF JOHAN GALTUNG[7]

The work of Johan Galtung, at present Professor of Peace Research at the University of Oslo and Director of the International Peace Research Institute in Oslo, has had a great influence on this country, especially through the ex-Lancaster group. In a recent publication Michael Banks[11] gives a brief summary of the work of Galtung, also mentioning some contributions by Robin Jenkins:

'Two of the leading writers currently exploring the problem of stating measurable dimensions for conflict are Galtung and Jenkins. Taken together, their work employs two of the truisms of international relations theory, rediscovered in conflict theory and combined with several sociological propositions. The truisms are, firstly, that the most fruitful approach to explaining behaviour in a conflict situation is not to take a Martian view but to study how the actor in the situation himself defines it. Perceptions, in short, are crucial. The second truism is that perception varies with the social distance from the problem. In common language this takes the form that the masses of the population tend to perceive a conflict situation in black and white absolute terms; they stress goals rather than means and emphasise the value aspects of the issue set. Decision-makers, high up the social scale, on the other hand, perceive the problem in gradualist terms, are more concerned with "rank" aspects (i.e. their interests and personal status), and worry much more about means to deal with the problem than the ethics of it. Stated in this way, and there is satisfactory empirical evidence to support both these generalisations, we come fairly close to saying that conflict in a subjective phenomenon. Where group action is concerned, what matters in a conflict situation is not so much the mass perceptions of the problem as an insoluble black and white dilemma but the much more subtle appreciation of the élites who see the more sophisticated difficulties of methods, consequences, and assorted interrelationships of any one problem with a host of others.'

However, if the subjective perceptions of élites are important to an understanding of conflict behaviour, it is necessary to understand the sources from which the conflict springs, and this requires a rather broader vision. Galtung therefore adds to these two preliminary truisms a fairly intricate set of sociological propositions in order to arrive at a model of conflict which yields a number of general conclusions. It is worth while considering these with some care. Galtung's latest statement of his theory starts from a wider definition of violence, similar to those that we have considered earlier. Thus, 'violence is present when human beings are influenced so that their actual somatic and mental realisations are below their potential realisations'. Once again we observe the unavoidability of the intrusion of the analyst's values. In fact Galtung admits that his definition has to be wide because otherwise, 'highly unacceptable social orders would still be compatible with peace'. Therefore, 'violence is here defined as the difference between the actual and the potential, between what could have been and what is'. And here, of course, we run into that old problem—how do we define people's potential? Under such a definition of violence as has been given to us by Galtung we can agree with Marcuse that a society which produces people whose actual realisations are confined to bingo and bad soap opera is a violent one.[16] However, such an argument is probably an academic quibble in view of the fact that in most of the social situations in which the conflict analyst is interested the relative deprivation would be readily apparent, and there would be some consensus that it exists as, for instance, in Vietnam or Ulster.

The more interesting distinctions come later. Galtung mentions that we think of violence in terms of some person doing something to some other person. Indeed, he maintains, such thinking is embedded in western language with its basic units of subject, verb, object. If we free ourselves from these distinctions we can see other analytic possibilities. The first of these is violence with no object; an example is a national or a tribal display of chauvinism. Such a phenomenon is of interest, first because it is potentially dangerous to some outside party, and secondly because it can have deleterious effects on those displaying it—it limits their possible achievements and warps their minds.

More important, though, is violence without a subject. In these cases it is impossible to pin down someone in terms of a person or a group responsible for the violence. An example would be the underachievement of working-class children in schools. We call this kind of violence 'structural'; it is built into the society.

What are the conditions that uphold such structural violence? 'Obviously just as military science and related subjects would be

c

indispensable to the understanding of personal violence, so is the science of social structure, particularly of stratification, indispensable to the understanding of structural violence.' Galtung then constructs his own generalised model of a social system. This has five basic components.

The *actor,* persons or groups who have goals and their pattern of interactions which are *systems* (any group or person may be involved in several systems). The total aggregate of interrelated systems forms the *structure.* But of course any such structure may be an actor at another social *level.* Finally the dimension of *rank* describes the position of the actors in the social structure, on various system dimensions.

Galtung then distinguishes six factors that serve to maintain inegalitarian distributions and consequently can be seen as mechanisms of structural violence.

1. **Linear ranking order.** In this case the ranking is complete, leaving no doubt as to who is higher in any pair of actors. The society thereby appears as an enormous chain of command.

2. **A cyclical pattern of interaction.** All the actors are connected but only one way. There is only one correct path of interaction. Such interactions will therefore be heavily in favour of those who have substantial interests in the *status quo.*

3. **High correlation between rank and centrality.** The higher the rank of the actor in the system, the more central his position is in the interaction network. The more central the position, the disproportionately higher is the influence of the actor. The best example of all this is the old adage describing organisations as a wheel. The actor in the middle can see all that goes on, while those out on the spokes can only see to one position on either side. The closer to the centre of the wheel, the higher is the actor, not only in his own system, but the greater are his chances of interaction with, and therefore influence over, other systems. (This would provide, for example, a good description of the position of the super-powers in world affairs.)

4. **Congruence between systems.** Here the interaction networks are structurally similar; this means that people with ability to climb one system can also climb others. For example, most middle-class professions require roughly the same characteristics.

5. **Concordance between the ranks.** If an actor is high in one system he tends automatically to be high in others. This means that the society contains an élite, a group of people who are highly ranked in all the major systems.

6. **High rank couplings between lives.** For example, if a man is elected mayor of a town he not only gains the influence in that town that goes with that position, but he also represents his town in the County Council which gives him even higher influence. In the same way a leading actor in an alliance may speak for that alliance in higher world councils, thus substantially increasing his influence.

The reader will have noticed that all these different combinations are what are generally regarded as different forms of necessary social organisation; necessary in order to attain the goals of any society. The point made by Galtung is that all these systems tend to move towards their extreme forms, which in each case are highly repressive and therefore violent. The task, then, is to work constantly against such 'social gravity'. Sooner or later, failure to work against it will result in manifest personal violence, and Galtung has shown us a social mechanism that will cause such changes. It is not the most polarised violent system that will change most rapidly; it is those where there is just enough flexibility for actors to be *rank disequilibrated*. That is, where a person who on one dimension is relatively high is refused status on others. Sure enough, we find that in Northern Ireland it was the middle-class Catholics who in the 1950s began to obtain higher positions on the financial ladder, but were denied status by the Protestant-dominated community, and the socially dominant Protestants who were low on wealth, who started the overt violence. Bernadette Devlin has a university education and Ian Paisley comes from a poor background. Such an analysis may also be applied to international relations. The state at present most feared by the *status quo* powers is China, high on population and new-found atomic strength, but accorded extremely low status by other members of the international system.

Galtung's hypothesis also accords well with the conventional historical wisdom that revolutions occur just when the quality of life is marginally improved for the lower classes, and also with the contention that British society has experienced a relatively low level of overt violence by allowing disenfranchised groups ready access to positions of relative social strength.

A final point is that when the disequilibrated actors have achieved rank concordance the process will start all over again. Thus the remedy is constant action on the broad social scale against such inequalities. Galtung, therefore, in many respects qualifies as a structuralist thinker, concerned with social engineering on a large scale. This is what most markedly differentiates

him from the other major school of thought led by John
Burton.

JOHN BURTON

Burton's position can best be explained by an examination of the
set of propositions with which he concludes his last book, *Systems,
States, Diplomacy and Rules.*[5] He starts by saying: 'Conflict within
states exists to the extent that the values of administrators and
groups take precedence over community values.' The point here
is that the political survival values held by administrative groups
and the sectional interests of different social groupings cannot
necessarily be considered to contribute to the 'common good'.
Burton extends this well-known proposition into the area of
interstate relations and says: 'Conflict between states exists to the
extent that the values of administrators, groups and communities
take precedence over the values of functional systems that embrace
more than one side.' At its simplest level, the contention here is
that the notion of the 'common good' could be applied to interstate relations. We must then ask in what lies this 'common good'.
The answer is that states conduct various transactions between
them, ranging from the exchange of people to the exchange of
goods and services. These transactions follow their own dynamic
and may often be considered self-adjusting. However, the authorities in various states may seek, for various reasons, to disrupt such
sets of transactions. For example, immigration and emigration
flows may be viewed in two ways. From one point of view they
are a natural flow from low to high income areas of population
over the world; another view derives from situations which
involve governments protecting their constituents from change
and setting up barriers. Immigration flows become 'immigration
problems', and a conflict flares up. It is in this sense that
one can talk of state authorities interfering with systems
transactions.

This is a main theme running through much of Burton's work.
Social life consists of continuous adaptation to social change and
Burton would argue that the correct role of political authorities
therefore is to expedite such change as smoothly as possible.
Government of this kind demands a close reciprocal relationship
with various sections of the community; a relationship that is
oriented towards problem-solving. However, the political system
has its own separate needs, which prevent the solution of these
kinds of problems—thus political authorities have to be con-

cerned with maintaining power and the boundaries within which their influence operates.

This leads to a second thesis in Burton's work. He maintains that if the use of power is solely confined to resisting change, it will in the long term be ineffective because in the modern world social change is both continuous and ubiquitous.

Both these problems, i.e. the inherent conflict between state authorities and systems transactions, and the constant social change set up by these transactions, are compounded by the fact that the unitarian political state is a myth. The majority of states in the world contain major social, cultural or geographical divisions. This often results in the state becoming a third party to conflicts with its territory. In such situations the opposed groups can very quickly become separate entities, as in Cyprus, Sudan and Biafra. The international significance of such phenomena is that intra-state fighting often becomes international because the internal groups appeal for external aid from parties with whom they are linked by those sets of systems transactions mentioned earlier. Indeed Burton claims that the vast majority of international conflicts since World War II have their origins in divisions inside the states concerned.

Overt violence in such situations is contagious in the international system because, according to Burton, 'demands for participation, or resistance to them, in one state attract support from those making similar demands or resisting them in other states'. This proposition brings us back to the idea that social conflict has its roots in social inequality. The only stable social order, both within the state or in its relationships with others, is one that is accepted by all the relevant actors and to which they are prepared to adjust. To ignore this axiom is to produce hostile reactions from other actors and, because of this, the defence of unacceptable social positions is eventually a self-destroying policy. Again we see a reflection of Galtung's contention that all unacceptable orders contain within themselves the seeds of their own destruction.

So the heart of the trouble lies in the need to adjust to change. 'Conflict is change, associated with systems failure to absorb or adjust passively to change.' In short, the more power an actor has at his disposal, the more able he is to force the consequences of change on others, like the employer who sacks his men in a falling market. Large and powerful states are therefore a source of conflict to the extent that they employ power as a means of forcing the burden of adjustment on others. Smaller powers are initiators of violence to the extent that they react against such power in positions that impede their progress and restrict their freedom of action. Thus far Burton's theoretical orientation approaches Galtung's in that it identifies those conditions in which social structures are likely to produce conflict.

The resemblance finishes there. The argument is developed that most social systems are in principle quite capable of carrying out the necessary readjustments for adapting to social change; the problems arise when political systems fail to cope and become unresponsive. A dominant theme of Burton's work on conflict resolution is that the social environment is multidimensional and provides enormous scope for the redistribution of costs and values, given the will and understanding of the relevant political parties. Thus, he states, 'whether functional conflict becomes dysfunctional depends upon decision-making processes'. In a rational world it would immediately be realised that any conflict between two parties which is likely to be dysfunctional for one party will also be dysfunctional for the other. This extends to the proposition that if any one party perceives a conflict as negative sum then it immediately becomes negative sum for all the other participants. If any party to a conflict cannot see this it is the result of false perceptions, false expectations and irrelevant responses.

Conflict is a situation where the involved parties are reaping the costs of past failures to adjust. John Burton's model of conflict is therefore fundamentally subjective. It is a descendant of the nineteenth-century school of thought which held that nature adjusted itself and that disharmonies only resulted when men tried to interfere with it. Once this is understood conflict disappears; and the 'resolution of conflict is possible when all parties agree that the conflict is non-functional'. The problem therefore becomes a question of designing a technique that will give parties an understanding of the nature of conflict and allow them to communicate between themselves effectively on the basis of this understanding.

CONTROLLED COMMUNICATION

Burton's greatest contribution to conflict research has been in the designing of just such a technique. The procedure is best described by him: 'Data are generated by bringing together persons nominated by, and in this sense representing the viewpoints of, governments or communities that are engaged in conflict. The data generating process of discussion in which the participants are parties in a dispute and a panel of social and political scientists with a special knowledge of international relations studies is itself a valuable insight. Great value also arises out of the preparation of relevant hypotheses and models prior to discussion and the continued observation of the conflict in its subsequent stages.' The technique therefore involves bringing participants in a conflict together into a mutual academic framework, and closely following their perceptions of the situation.

If, as we saw above, the resolution of conflict cannot rest on outside determination, and must come from the parties by processes that alter their perception and understandings of each other's viewpoints, then the re-establishment of communication is a basic precondition. If one assumes that conflicts between states are based on misperceptions, false calculations of costs, failure to perceive alternative means of obtaining goals and other such behavioural factors, the positive sum nature of conflict resolution becomes apparent. There can be mutual gain in resolving all conflicts.

'However, the problem is not to re-establish communication so much as to control it once re-established. Communication between parties by itself does not solve conflict; on the contrary it was communication that made the conflict possible and frequently re-established communication merely increases conflict. The form of the communication and the behaviour of the parties during communication determine its outcome.'

A third party is therefore required to control communication. The resolution of conflict depends on its accurate analysis, and while this can finally be made only by the parties themselves, they can make it only with whatever insight might be made available to them about the behaviour of states and the sociology of conflict. The function of the third party is to supply these, and for this reason members of this party must be specialists, familiar with theories concerning the behaviour of states and the various aspects of conflict.

It would not be putting it too highly to state that this is the first vehicle of conflict research which presents analysis and resolution and carries such information straight to the practitioners in a situation with the eventual aim of resolving conflict. As such it marks an important milestone in the theory of conflict.

CONCLUSION

In this chapter we have surveyed the broad compass of conflict research and also concentrated on two main pillars of its theory. Such an approach is bound to be superficial and is intended only to introduce the reader to the broad nature of the thinking in the discipline. This said, it is only fair to point out that most of the active research being undertaken in the field is much more tightly defined than that presented in this chapter, and represents a combination of most of the approaches.

Having set out the broad patterns of conflict theory, it is now possible to engage in a more rigorous analysis of the Ulster conflict. As a necessary precondition to an analytic survey we must first survey the history of that particular conflict situation.

[1] Anatole Rapaport, *Fights, Games and Debates*, University of Michigan Press, 1960.

[2] L. F. Richardson, *Arms and Insecurity*, Stevens, 1960.

[3] Michael B. Nicholson, *The Study of Conflict*, English Universities Press, 1970.

[4] This problem is taken up in greater detail in Chapter 5.

[5] J. W. Burton, *Systems, States, Diplomacy and Rules*, Cambridge University Press, 1968.

[6] A. N. Oppenheim and J. C. R. Bayley in *Proceedings of Third I.P.R.A. Conference*, 1969.

[7] Johan Galtung, 'A structural theory of aggression', *Journal of Peace Research*, ii, 1964; 'Institutionalized conflict resolution', *Journal of Peace Research*, iv, 1965; 'International relations and international conflicts: a sociological approach', in *Transactions of the Sixth World Congress of Sociology*, 1966; 'Rank and social integration', in Joseph Berger *et al*, eds. *Sociological Theories in Progress* (Houghton Mifflin, 1966); 'Violence, peace and peace research', *Journal of Peace Research*, iv, 1969.

[8] Lewis A. Coser, *Continuities in the Study of Study of Social Conflict*, New York, Free Press; London, Collier Macmillan, 1967.

[9] Robin Jenkins, 'Conflict and polarization', *Sociology*, 1968.

[10] *The Essays of A. J. Muste*, ed. Nat Hentoff, Indianapolis, Bobbs-Merril, 1967; see pp. 179–85.

[11] Michael Banks, *Conflict: Behavioural Approaches and their Relevance to the Settlement of International Disputes*, Centre for the Analysis of Conflict (mimeographed).

[12] David Easton, *A Systems Analysis of Political Life*, Wiley, 1965; Oran R. Young, *Systems of Political Science*, Prentice-Hall, 1968; Charles A. Maclelland, *Theory and the International System*, Macmillan of New York, 1966; *Yearbook of the Society for General Systems Research* (Annual).

[13] For an outline of the vocabulary of systems theory see: Oran R. Young, 'A survey of general systems theory', *General Systems*, vol. ix, 1964.

[14] Ross W. Ashby, *Design for a Brain*, Chapman and Hall, 1952.

[15] K. W. Deutsche, *The Nerves of Government*, New York, Free Press; London, Macmillan, 2nd edn., 1966 (particularly ch. 5).

[16] Herbert Marcuse, *One Dimensional Man*, Sphere Books, 1964 (see, for example, p. 23).

2

Background to the conflict in Ulster

UP TO 1963

In this chapter we give a brief history of Ulster and a description of the social background and main institutions involved in the present conflict. It should be emphasised at the outset that the aim is not to give a comprehensive history of Northern Ireland, which has been done extremely well elsewhere.[1] It is only our purpose to provide sufficient material to put the reader in context.

Ireland as a whole is a nation of intensely strong loyalties and this is particularly true of the Six Counties. Even the most naïve visitor cannot fail to notice the strong evidence given by the Protestant community of loyalty to the British constitution and flag and way of life, and by the Catholic community of belonging to the Irish nation. Public parades, flag flying and a garrulous tradition of public oratory all ensure that these loyalties remain overt. Such fierce loyalties derive from the unique historical background of Ulster. History is very much a part of the present in Northern Ireland: discussions of massacres and battles, political pogroms that took place two or three hundred years ago, are a part of the everyday language of the Ulsterman. When one of the authors was interviewing in Northern Ireland during the fighting in Londonderry, he quite often heard comparisons made between fighting of the day before and some other battle whose name he did not recognise, only later to discover that reference was being made to battles fought two or three hundred years previously. Obviously, a sense of opposition and trust in one's own community is deeply bound up with this sense of history. In order to grasp this, some attention must be paid to the past of Northern Ireland.

Ever since the Gallic invasions of 1 B.C. Ireland has been constantly invaded, not least because of a tradition of political disunification covering the whole island. In the twelfth century Ireland was divided into different kingdoms, each jealously resisting any infringement of its own territory. This is not to say that there was no Irish entity as such; its relative isolation from Europe, particularly in religious terms, earned it the title of 'The Island of Saints and Scholars'. It was in fact just this isolation from the mainstream of European political life that enabled Henry II in 1171 to gain Papal approval for the establishment of English ascendancy in Ireland. For the Catholic community this represents the beginning of 750 years of foreign rule, although in Northern Ireland English control was, for long periods, virtually negligible. By the mid-fourteenth century, for example, England had very little power in either Ulster or Connaught.

The problem for the English monarchy was that the ascendancy was always endangered by English overlords becoming integrated with the Irish community. Thus in 1366 the Statutes of Kilkenny established a form of apartheid, formalising the distinction between the Irish and the English Churches and forbidding inter-marriage between English and Irish. However, the intermingling continued and out of it came a tradition involving a dominance by the great Anglo-Irish families. This loose liaison between English and Irish came to an end in 1543 when Henry VIII was crowned King of Ireland. This single act committed the English to a colonial type of situation in northern Ireland where settlers were introduced, whom the Crown had to defend against encroachments by the Irish. The reign of Queen Elizabeth was notable in this respect; she began the plantation of Ireland, bringing in Scots and English into Counties Antrim and Down in order to establish English supremacy. In 1641 under Charles I there was a large Irish uprising in Ulster, which resulted in widespread massacre. Eight years afterwards, in 1649, Cromwell came to Ireland and took his revenge by expelling more Catholic Irish and establishing more English Protestant settlers.

Ireland, and in particular northern Ireland, was therefore constantly plagued by the vagaries of English politics. This was especially apparent when James II, in his attempt to restore Catholic influence in England, lost his throne and in 1689 fled to Ireland. On his arrival the Dublin Parliament passed an Act confiscating the estates of over 2000 Protestant landlords. The Siege of Londonderry and the Battle of the Boyne in 1690 ended any Irish hopes of Catholic ascendancy in northern Ireland and left a bitter heritage of religious strife. After the Battle of the Boyne there were thousands of exiles and confiscations, and English rule in Ulster became a stranglehold.

Even now the split between the two communities was not complete. There were differences amongst the Protestant community inside Ireland, particularly between Anglicans and Dissenters, and in 1771 Societies of United Irishmen were formed in Belfast and Dublin, which gave institutional expression to the emerging alliance between Catholic and Dissenter. The 1789 Irish socialist uprising, sparked off by the French Revolution, ended this, and repolarised all Protestants against Catholics. (In addition, in 1795 formal Orange Lodges were first formed to maintain the laws and peace of the country and to protect the Protestant constitution.) In 1800 the Irish Parliament was abolished and direct rule instituted from Westminster.

British rule thereafter was oppressive and shortsighted. Refusal to cut tariffs at the time of the 1845 potato famine and to take action against the widespread absenteeism of landlords created further bitterness. However, the fact that Ireland was now controlled from Westminster allowed discussion of the possibility of Home Rule which would have never been possible in an Ireland where there was only a Protestant voice. By 1880 there was discussion in the English Parliament of Home Rule on reforming grounds. But the concept of Home Rule for all Ireland overlooked the firm links between the Protestant élite in Ulster and industry in Great Britain—a connection that was fostered by the Conservative Party. In 1886 there was communal rioting in Ulster against Home Rule. The Conservatives played the Ulster card; it was Randolph Churchill who said, 'Ulster will fight and Ulster will be right.' Owing to various political circumstances there was insufficient support for a Home Rule bill in the House of Commons until 1910. However, in that year Irish members held the balance at Westminster and it was possible to go ahead with Home Rule for at least part of Ireland. But the years between the late 1880s and 1910 had given birth to increased bitterness inside Ireland; the Fenians and Sinn Fein became active in their campaign for a united and independent Ireland. Also in the South James Connolly had led a movement for a socialist, united country. The bogey of socialism, which is still not entirely dead, played in Ireland much the same role as communism in most of the colonial world since 1945. On the other side of the intercommunal split, half a million Protestants had by 1912 subscribed to a Solemn League and Covenant and the Ulster Volunteer Force had been formed to fight for Ulster's independence. The lines drawn by this time were rigid and bitter.

To the further detriment of intercommunal relations the war of 1914–18 delayed the granting of independence to Ireland. During the war southern Ireland gave support to the German cause and it was then that the slogan 'England's danger is Eire's opportunity' was coined. Thus along with a history of colonial feuding and accusations of socialist influence there was now the grudge engendered by accusations of treachery. By 1921 when the Constitution of free Ireland was signed, allowing for an independent six counties in the North, the split was irrevocable. The Catholics in the North refused to participate in Ulster politics, perceiving themselves to be unfairly placed among an English-supported Protestant majority. On the other hand the Protestant majority felt like an embattled community in the midst of a hostile Catholic Ireland. Small wonder, then, that the provision for a Grand Parliament of Ireland to coordinate the affairs of the Eire Government and the Ulster Government was never realised.

SOCIAL BACKGROUND OF THE CONFLICT

It is impossible, as always, to try and decide the rights and wrongs of the conflict from an inspection of the historical data; nevertheless several things are apparent. The first is that there is a long legacy of strife from which both sides can draw ammunition to support their own cases. Not only do they draw on different events but each side has a different interpretation of the same events. For the Catholics most of the period of English rule represented outright colonial repression. For the Protestants it was a noble attempt on the part of the English Parliament to support a besieged but civilising community inside Ireland. Again, Connolly's socialism was probably a natural response to the repressive tactics adopted by Protestant landlords, most of whom were resident in England. To the Protestants it represented only a development of the cancer of the French Revolution. Lastly the aid given by the Southern Irish community to the Central powers during the First World War could not be accepted by loyalist Protestants. The Southerners saw it only as a vindication of their inalienable right to choose their own side in war.

The conflict was made the more intractable since the hostility and opposition fell along well demarcated social and cultural lines. There was a gulf between the two social structures as well as between cultural beliefs. It is difficult for an Englishman to understand the extent to which such differences can affect two communities' perceptions of each other. Groups in a plural society may be marked by various differences, only some of which strike us as natural grounds for mutual opposition. For example,

the Greek and Turkish communities in Cyprus have different
religions, which means that they end up with different rules about
marriage, diet and inheritance; they also have different languages.
They have hundreds of years of political contact and opposition.
The only obvious difference they do not have is physical appearance. The Ulster situation is in many ways similar. Although the
English language is used by both groups, the Irish language and
the illegal tricolour flag is something special to many Catholics.
From the religious differences come crucial rules about marital
and sexual behaviour, and dietary rules. An awareness of Cromwell's massacres at Drogheda and Wexford and of the decisive
Protestant victory at the Boyne is socialised into school children
and it becomes as much a part of the consciousness of belonging
to each faith as being black is for an American Negro. The fact
that such aspects of group identity are invisible does not make
them any the less powerful in determining lines of cooperation
and cleavage.

Even where differences between groups seem quite trivial to
outsiders, to participants they may be crucial. In the Mediter-
ranean countryside people often speak of the next village or the
upper part or the lower part of a town as if the dwellers there
illustrated an encyclopaedia of the vices. Not only are they the
biggest liars, cheats, thieves and cuckolds, but they also sleep
with their sisters. Sometimes there is a traditional annual confrontation between the villagers or the town sections which leads
to fights, just as often and inevitably as do Ulster parades. Boys
who come from the other place are beaten up if they try to court
local girls, obscene rhymes are invented and sung lustily on feast
days. With all the apparent hostility, the curious thing is that
people actually are pretty civil to each other when they meet. Such
opposition probably plays a part in damping down hostility within
the community; the moral characteristics attributed to the enemy
group are plainly untrue, there is a level at which people know
they are not describing their neighbours accurately, but at times
they act on the information they know to be inaccurate.

What we are describing here is a situation where two communities eventually end up needing their mutual opposition in order to
maintain their own values and beliefs about themselves. It is also
a situation where a multitude of different little signals serve to
make the native aware of the foreignness of a member of the
opposite community. In such a situation political interdependence
and geographical proximity become factors which militate
towards danger. It is true that both communities have to develop
rules which allow them to live together in the normal course of

events, whether they be rules concerning the allocation of rewards in the political system or how one addresses a member of the Protestant community at the local shop. However, this is a very different kind of coexistence from that which, for example, people from Yorkshire have with people from Lancashire. In the Ulster situation any interdependence the two communities may have (and at the most basic level they depend on each other if only to keep the peace) becomes a matter of vulnerability. It is always important not to expose one's weaker points; one must always keep one's defences up. In such a situation, given the perspectives held by the two communities, it is rational to maintain a defensive and suspicious posture towards the other side. In the British press we often read editorials which state that the situation in Ulster would be completely calm if only the two sides could be more rational about their behaviour towards each other. Such statements overlook the subjective nature of rationality. The Protestant feels he is faced with a threatening Papist conspiracy and the possibility of a repressive rule by a Catholic majority in a united Ireland. In this light, his tactics with regard to maintaining his influence, status and prestige in Northern Ireland are entirely rational, the more so since the people against whom he is defending his position appear to him in every way foreign.

Such relationships take on the nature of self-fulfilling prophesies —the other side is treated as hostile and aggressive and therefore responds in that fashion, precisely because the other side is also keeping up its guard. Almost any move the other side makes is treated with suspicion: if the other side tries to increase its autonomy or become more independent, this is regarded as a threat. A Catholic-controlled free Londonderry would be a decided threat to the Protestant ascendancy, and any attempt to establish such a political situation would meet with extreme resistance from the Protestant side. If either community looks elsewhere for aid it is immediately accused of seeking imperialist help. Thus when the Ulster Irish look for help from the Catholics in the South the Protestant ascendancy treats this as one more proof of their seeking to overthrow the Constitution of Northern Ireland. When the Ulster Protestants look to Britain for help to the Catholics this is one more indication of the fact that the Protestant Irish are a small minority supported by an imperial power. This atmosphere makes it almost impossible for the two sides to negotiate meaningfully, even if there were this intention on either side. However, in global terms, this almost exhausts the possibilities of the different relationships that the two communities might have between themselves. If they cannot increase their autonomy, or look elsewhere for help, or negotiate with each other, the only option that they have left is to attack each other. This is of course a vast simplification, but it may, nevertheless, turn out to be a true description of recent events.

Of course, the disparity in size is also crucial. It allows both sides to feel embattled: the Catholics against the Protestant majority in Northern Ireland and the Protestants against the Catholic majority in the whole island. In terms of the situation inside Ulster it leads to a deadly cycle. Because the Catholic community is small and vulnerable, it is concerned primarily with its own security. The Protestant community is not so much concerned with its security as with control over the whole of Protestant Ulster. In simplified terms, what happens when both sides try to make a deal? If the Protestants make an offer that they perceive to be generous, how will it be received by the Catholic community? First, it will be treated with extreme suspicion; the reaction from a community that fears for its security is one of wait and see; it is up to the larger side to make concessions. However, such a response is only likely to build up pressure on the larger side, because there is always a group of people who can say there was never any point in making concessions in the first place, and that the lack of response from the smaller community bears this out. This inhibits the chances of making further concessions and also makes sure that the next reaction from the majority community will be all the more violent. This is a syndrome that has been only too apparent in Cyprus in recent years. It was also readily observable in Northern Ireland over the course of 1969 and 1970. Every time the Protestant community made any concessions, they were never enough for the Catholic minority, yet every concession made by the Protestant side was used as ammunition by the Protestant militants for vowing they would make no more.

Thus the two communities, loaded with a long history of mutual opposition, are also faced with a situation where there is a very low level of information flowing between them, which only alienates them further. As we have mentioned, there are rules which govern the day to day relationships between the two sides, but should there be any substantial shift in the social balance, or should anything happen to upset those rules, then there is every reason to be pessimistic about the future of such a society. As we explain later in this chapter, it was just such a shift in the social situation and just such a breakdown of the rules between the two communities which led to the violence which erupted in 1969, and will probably lead to worse violence in the years to come.

We must now survey, at least in the broad outline, the social institutions of Ulster in order to talk more accurately about the relationships between the two communities.

The dominant political party is the Unionist Party which also sends members to Westminster. The party has had a majority in Parliament ever since the foundation of the state. Until 1968, 70 per cent of the election contests were not even fought inside safe Unionist constituencies. It is the party of Protestants, firmly established in the sectarian split between the two communities. Because of this it includes a broad compass of political opinion amongst the Protestant community. It is wrong to describe the Protestant party as uniformly intolerant and repressive. For example, it had no trouble coping with the 1945 English Labour Government policy which it for the most part re-enacted. It has in fact only one firm policy of its own and this is loyalty to the British Crown, to which everything else must be subordinated. However, the breadth of its membership means that the party must come under considerable strain in times of crisis, as indeed it did over the course of 1968 and 1969. In 1969, for example, there were independent O'Neill Unionist candidates standing at the polls against the official Unionist candidates. With the drift of certain sections of the party to the right there is a growing possibility that the Unionist Party could split down the middle since it is difficult to see how it can contain such divergences of opinion. The Unionist Party is therefore the social institution that wields the symbols and trappings of Protestant dominance in Northern Ireland. However, up to the time of writing, the institution that wields the power of Protestant dominance has been the Orange Order.

Until the end of the eighteenth century the Orange Order was a Protestant peasant association. As such it was not exclusively linked with the Protestant hierarchy; there are records of Orange Order Protestant peasants turning Protestant landlords out of their property and re-renting it to Irish Catholics at a low rate. Wolfe Tone succeeded in forging the Protestant/Orange Order Alliance, and after the early nineteenth century there was no mutually beneficial interaction as such between the Order and the Catholic community. But the link between Orange Order and Protestant power was not solidified until this century, when the Order's two senior lodges, the Apprentice Boys of Derry and the Royal Black Preceptory, were infiltrated by the landed and business classes of the Protestant community. Access to political and commercial influence made the Orange Order a powerful institution which was able and willing to distribute patronage in return for loyalty. Since then the Orange system has had an important apparatus running through all levels of Protestant social organisation. At the local level it covers what jobs go to its members, is heavily engaged in local politics and is also instrumental in providing the necessary manpower for discouraging resistance to its influence. At the national level the Order has significant influence in the Unionist Party. The County Grand Lodges nominate 105 of the members of the Unionist Council. All the members of the Government are members of the Order. The nephew of the Prime Minister was expelled from it for attending a Catholic marriage in the cause of good communal relations. The fact that Captain O'Neill, during his leadership's period of crisis, required votes of confidence from the Orange Order as well as from the Unionist Party is some indication of the Order's influence. It is nearly impossible to be a Unionist candidate without Orange membership. The Order stands far to the right of the mainstream of the Unionist Party and generally has greatest influence in times of crisis when people tend to perceive issues in fundamentalist terms. In many respects the 'B' Specials could be described as the strong arm of the Orange Order, and their formal disbanding is no guarantee that the same individuals will not continue to perform the same services for the Order.

On the Catholic side the Ancient Order of Hibernians is a pale shadow of the Orange Order structure. However, because of the Catholic retreat from Ulster politics in 1921 and the political view taken by the Church of Ireland in Ulster, it has never had the same power as the Orange Order. One should also note that the Hibernians have no access to the sort of patronage enjoyed by the Orange Order. It is, nevertheless, feared by the Protestants since, like the Orange Order, it controls a large part of the social activities of the members of its community; worship, sport, social meetings and business all tend to cluster round these institutions.

The Nationalist Party is the biggest opposition party to the Unionists in the Parliament House at Stormont. However, deprived of political power, and representing a community disenchanted with Northern politics, it is more an association of MPs than a party. Just as, over the years, the Catholic community reconciled itself to the existence of the border, so the opposition of the Nationalists in Parliament became no more than token opposition. The Party thus earned for itself the title of 'Green Tories', and, in the eyes of many Catholics, Eddie McAteer, their leader until 1969, earned the kiss of death when many Unionists described him as a responsible opposition leader.

If any Ulster party can claim to be non-sectarian it is the

D

Northern Ireland Labour Party. This is a party with MPs in Westminster and fairly good connections with the British Labour Party. However, because of the absence of class politics in Ulster, it has gained little support outside Belfast. It obtains much of its financial support from the Ulster trade unions, which also present themselves as an unbiased party. Their success in this derives partly from the fact that they make a point of saying very little about sectarian politics. Moreover, Catholics and Protestants tend to work in different branches of the same unions. While such tacit discrimination is hardly encouraging, it is noticeable that the Belfast docks experienced very little trouble in the 1969 rioting.

The only Catholic community party that managed to retain its bite between 1921 and 1968 was the Republican Labour Party; it has two members in Stormont and one member in Westminster. A large part of its financial support is derived from expatriate Irish in the United States. (Incidentally the amount of revenue flowing in to all sides from American Irish is probably quite high; unfortunately there are no data on this financial intervention. It is an area worthy of research.) For reasons we have given in connection with the other Catholic parties, the support obtained by the Republican Labour Party has been very small. It has been easily discredited in Protestant eyes by associating it with that all-purpose bogey man, the Irish Republican Army. The last period of armed activity by the IRA was between 1958 and 1961 when they conducted an armed campaign against the Ulster Constitution. Since 1961 the IRA has not been in favour of military activity but has taken on a Marxist tinge and prefers to pursue its goals by political means. This was dramatically illustrated by the low level of IRA activity in the North during the fighting late in 1969. According to apocryphal rumour they were seriously embarrassed by the fact that they had previously given away most of their guns to the Free Wales Army. The recent (February 1970) attempts of the IRA to find arms in Great Britain may bear out this rumour. However, they continue to fulfil their purpose as a bogy, thus leaving the Republican Labour Party with little room for manoeuvre.

For reasons we describe later in this chapter, the significant parties in the recent situation have been new. On the Catholic side, the Civil Rights Association started its activities in the early 1960s. It was initially a group of middle-class Catholics who by normal political pressures sought to gain equal rights for their community. Initially they cooperated with some of the small middle-class groups which contained some members from each community, such as the New Ulster Movement, PACE and the

Campaign for Social Democracy. This moderate approach, as we show later, was to prove of little avail, and the group broadened and moved further to the left and into the realm of direct action. In this it was supported by the People's Democracy, a group mostly of radical students from both communities centred on Queen's University. Because of the increasing polarisation brought about by the troubles of 1969, the People's Democracy was forced back into the Catholic community. Its members are certainly radical but it is doubtful whether they are really 'The Tools of the Third Chinese Communist International', as some members of the Unionist Government maintain. On the Protestant side, the emergence of the protesting Catholic middle-class groups created a backlash known as Paisleyism. Ian Paisley, a Moderator of the Free Presbyterian Church, ably assisted by Major Ronald Bunting, brought into being the Ulster Constitution Defence Committee. Paisley's group is fundamentalist and loyalist; it rests on overt support from the Protestant working class and a great deal of tacit support from the Protestant middle and upper classes.

Such are the main social institutions in Northern Ireland. Having briefly surveyed them, the next logical step is to survey the social processes. In this section we will concentrate on religion, politics— national and local, social relations, employment and housing.

The centrality of religion in Ulster should by now be apparent, but its degree is surprising when one considers the census figures reproduced below.

	1951	*1961*[4]
Roman Catholic	471,460	498,031
Presbyterian	410,215	413,006
Church of Ireland	353,245	344,584
Methodist	66,639	71,912

The results of the 1961 census reveal that of the total population of Northern Ireland only sixty-four people profess themselves to be atheists.

The doctrinal differences between the Protestant and Roman (Catholic Churches need not be recounted here. However, doctrinal influences are heavily emphasised in the context of inter-communal opposition, as the following quotation should indicate. It is a letter from the General Secretary of the Christian Fellowship Centre and Irish Emancipation Crusade, to the *Belfast Newsletter* 4 November 1964):

We desire to place on record our deep dismay and sorrow at the proposed visit to the Pope by his Grace the Archbishop

of Canterbury. This is indeed a grievous blow to our evangelical position, and a step which will inevitably draw the judg-
ment of God on Church and State. We would call upon
Christian people in all our Churches to devote themselves
increasingly to prayer. We need delude ourselves no longer.
The die is cast—the step has been taken. The most we can do
now is to pray for courage and faith, that we might be true to
the simplicity of the gospel in this dark hour and in the darker
days that lie before us.

We respectfully suggest that in those Churches and Mission
Halls where evangelical truth is still cherished, the national
anthem should be sung as a prayer next Sunday, with the
congregation and minister kneeling in the attitude of prayer.

At the popular level, doctrinal differences manifest themselves in
prolific slogan writing. Such epigrams as 'Jesus saves, the Pope
enslaves' are common. Along with doctrinal differences go varia-
tions in social custom and practice that differentiate all religions.
Catholics are prepared to indulge in Sunday entertainment which
is regarded by the Protestants as being nearly as wicked as the
Pope's position on birth control. From the Catholic point of view
the Protestant faith is dour and draped with the trappings of
middle-class morality.

Along with doctrinal and habitual differences goes considerable
ignorance of the opposite community's religion. The Protestants
generally overestimate the unity of the Catholic Church, which is
often represented as a Popish conspiracy, emanating from Rome.
They point to social conditions in Spain, Colombia and Eire and
argue that Catholic domination can only mean repression. The
fact that no Catholic chaplain has ever been attached to the House
at Stormont is regarded as sure proof of this conspiracy.

Catholic fears centre not so much on the Protestant religions as
on the Protestant political and social domination. Nevertheless,
the fact that the (Anglican) Church of Ireland in particular shares
much of its formal worship with, and participates in the apparatus
of, the Orange Order is for them a token of its domination. There
is much misunderstanding here. What to the Catholic side looks
like an intended Protestant conspiracy, is for many Protestant
mothers merely a method of keeping their boys off the streets.

In the political sphere the Protestant ascendancy is symbolised
by the firm grip of the Unionist Party over the machinery of
national government. It should be pointed out that at the national
level there is no evidence of gerrymandering in favour of the
Protestant community. (Of course one may regard the border as

the biggest gerrymander of all.) Like British Liberals, the Catholic community generally tends to argue in favour of proportional representation, pointing out that Unionist M.P.s can hardly claim to represent effectively the sometimes significant Catholic minorities in their constituencies.

At the national level, there has only been one dominating issue: the existence or otherwise of the state and its connection with Great Britain. The Unionist Party campaigns on this platform in all its general elections; until recently it has had no other political programme at all except for the step by step policy of re-enacting British statutes in the House at Stormont, including the latest sets of reforms which were forced on the Unionist Government by Westminster. While it is fair to point to the electoral justice of the system of government in Northern Ireland, such a description gives little indication of the frustration it causes to the Catholic community. Parliamentary procedure consists of passing Unionist bills, and, until recently, of listening to the Opposition in a bored fashion. Only one Opposition Bill has ever been passed by the House and this was to do with the conservation of natural wild life.

The political realities most pertinent to the Ulsterman are those of local government. It is from positions of local government that patronage in the form of housing and jobs is most effectively controlled. It is also at this level that Protestant control is maintained by the use of the gerrymander, the existence of which is now substantiated. The most obvious example is Londonderry which until 1969 had a Unionist majority on the Council while only 37 per cent of the population were Protestants. Gerrymandering takes place in Strabane, Dungannon, Downpatrick, Enniskillen and several other towns in southern Ulster. However, the argument is not so cut and dried as the democratic Englishman might imagine. Its lines follow a pattern with which nineteenth-century England would have been familiar. The Protestant community maintains that democracy is more than the mere counting of heads. Those who own the most property, who pay the highest rates and contribute most to the running of the towns should have the dominant vote at the local political level. The Catholic community, of course, retorts that this is not democracy. For most Protestants the property view of democracy is sincerely held. The fact that they will state this view so blandly, generally serves only to enrage the Catholics further. It is also important to emphasise the relevance of local political history. In each town there is a long memory of previous grudges and debts to be settled, sets of intricate agreements concerning the flying of flags, the routing of marchers, the limits of acceptable police action, and so on. In general, disturbance at the national level tends to set up pressures which could destroy the delicate stand-off achieved at the local level.

In the sphere of social relations the two communities generally tend to remain well separated. In both the towns and the country-side the two communities are geographically separated for histori-cal reasons. In the towns the Protestants tended to live within the walls and the Catholics outside, and in the countryside the Protestant settlers took the rich lowlands and forced the Catholic population up to the more arid hill soil. Such differences tend to perpetuate themselves. Communities have their own shops and entertainments in particular areas. There are marked differences in the economic status between the two communities (see chart below).

Employment by occupation (our own survey in Portadown, 1960)[4]

	Catholic	Presby-terian	Church of Ireland	Metho-dist
Approximate percent-age of total labour force in:				
Professional, execu-tive, administrative occupations	1	5	6	7
Supervisory and lower managerial occupations	12	19	18	14
Skilled manual and routine non-manual work	32	50	43	58
Semi-skilled manual work	39	23	24	13
Unskilled work	16	3	9	8
	100	100	100	100

The fact of discrimination in employment once again is not in doubt, but its strength and direction are difficult to ascertain. When it has the chance the Catholic community discriminates as hard as does the Protestant one. The arguments surrounding discrimination in employment are complex, but they do not need reviewing here. The English reader should be familiar with all the points for and against made by the protagonists in the race relations debate in this country; the arguments are the same. The practice of discrimination also extends to housing. The National Northern Ireland Housing Trust does not discriminate. However, until 1969 the allocation of housing was in the hands of the local government authorities who did discriminate, as we shall see later in the chapter. It was in fact housing discrimination that set off the chain of events which led to the rioting of 1969.

Lastly, except at university level, the education systems for the two communities are completely separate, thus from childhood precluding any common view of history or politics.

One should emphasise that all these features of separation and discrimination are largely self-perpetuating. The reader may find it helpful here to refer back to the analysis in Chapter 1 of Johan Galtung's work on different patterns of social injustice inside society. The connection between latent and overt violence does not seem so abstract when studied in reality.

We have painted a picture of a polarised society. One may enquire why it is that change and conflict occurred in the 1960s rather than at any other particular time. As we discuss this in our analysis of the field work we undertook in Northern Ireland, a few brief comments should suffice here. First, we have indicated earlier the fact that Ireland's history follows a distinctly colonial pattern. One analyst has used this to describe changes in Ireland in recent times. [2] He points to the restricted authority of the Ulster Government, its powers in economic, defence and foreign matters are severely limited by Westminster. British markets account for 55 per cent of the gross national product of Ulster; the most rapid growth points in Ulster's economy are British subsidiaries; even the welfare services are run by United Kingdom subsidies. The fatal lack of power of a government with no substantial military arm has been dramatically demonstrated in recent years. Such a position is familiar from the case of many ex-Colonial governments, as is the fact that many such governments have relied on the use of the cry of 'the state in danger' in order to retain their power. Sectarian strife, it is argued, may be the weapon which keeps the Unionist Party in power. If the conflict were to split up along class lines, Unionist dominance would disappear over night.

The power of the indigenous élites in Ulster has been weakened by the introduction of British economic influence. The old landed élite lose power as the agricultural sector contracts (by 1966 agriculture counted for only 9·4 per cent of the gross domestic product). The old industrial élite controlled linen and shipping. In Ulster these two industries account for 23 per cent of employment, while in Great Britain they account for only 9·4 per cent. So the dominance of the élites is slipping. That is stage two of the argument. We have, therefore, an effectively weak government and an élite losing its influence. Such a situation would cause at least a certain amount of frustration, which could only be accentuated by the third factor described in this argument: that intrusive British industry allowed upward movement for the Catholic middle class and British employers were reluctant to discriminate on religious grounds against them. Thus the first protest in the Sixties came from middle-class Catholics asking for equality of status. At the same time, after 1964 the British Labour Government started putting pressure on Stormont to reform. The situation became explosive. In Galtung's terms, the Catholics were a disequilibrated group, who were allowed a certain amount of economic upward mobility, but denied the commensurate social status. If the emergence of this group provided the occasion for violence, the other disequilibrated group, the poor Protestants, provided its use. Paisleyism took a firm hold after 1967. The analysis is simplified, but is at least initially plausible. Just how plausible it is, the reader may decide for himself by inspecting the chain of events leading up to the 1969 and 1970 violence.

1963 TO 1966

The 23rd of March 1963 marked a new era. Lord Brookeborough had to resign on grounds of ill health; the Cabinet formed by his successor, Captain O'Neill, differed only slightly. There had been some mild opposition to Lord Brookeborough led by Mr Warroughk over the holding of some Government contracts by a firm in which a member of the Senate held a directorship. On 25 June 1963 Captain O'Neill introduced before the House at Stormont a Code of Conduct for Ministers, thus closing the controversy over business interests held by ministers in the Cabinet. This was to cause some disturbance in the future and it is worth taking note of Captain O'Neill's reform at that time.

The first real signs of a new direction in Government policy under Captain O'Neill came when he and Mr Lemass, the Prime Minister of the Irish Republic, held a meeting in Belfast on 14 January 1964, the first such meeting since the state of Northern Ireland was created in 1922. Throughout the Unionist Party, objections were raised, not least because the meeting had been kept a close secret and was not announced beforehand by the Prime Minister, even to the Northern Ireland Cabinet. The meeting took place at Stormont, the House of Commons in

Ulster, at one p.m. and continued at a luncheon afterwards. After the meeting the following communiqué was issued: 'We have discussed matters in which there may prove to be a degree of common interest, and we have agreed to explore further what specific measures may be possible or desirable by way of practical consultation and cooperation. Our talks, which did not touch upon constitutional or political matters, have been conducted in a most amicable way and we look forward to a future discussion in Dublin.' It is worth noting the reservation with regard to constitutional and political matters. Captain O'Neill must have realised the opposition that was likely to be focused against such a meeting from inside Ulster by those who had held up Southern Ireland as an implacable enemy of the state.

Mr Lemass also said in a later individual communiqué that his meeting had been fully in accord with the statement he had made earlier in the Republican Parliament; that the Government and Parliament in Belfast 'exists with the support of the majority in the Northern Ireland area, artificial though that area is'. Captain O'Neill later revealed that a set of low level meetings had been planned to discuss specific projects, and also explained that the meeting had been arranged informally through Mr Whittacker, the Eire representative at the World Bank. There was considerable overt public support expressed for the meeting on both sides of the border, but it also caused a considerable amount of unrest in certain sections of the Unionist Party, who were, as we have said, particularly annoyed about the lack of prior consultation with the Cabinet. The meeting marked a fundamental new direction in the relations between the two Governments, so badly strained after the period of the I.R.A. attacks.

On 9 February Captain O'Neill and Mr Lemass had a second meeting, this time in Dublin. They said once again that the talks had been cordial and that arrangements had been made for further contact. They also announced that in the meantime Mr Lynch and Mr Faulkner, the respective Ministers of Commerce, had held meetings on the promotion of trade and Irish goods. That there was a large area of functional cooperation cannot be doubted, and it would be interesting to trace the progress of the tentative plans that were laid then.

On 25 November 1963 general elections were held in Northern Ireland and the Unionists were returned with a majority of twenty seats. The elections were interesting in so far as they brought forward the first set of returns which showed some indication of increased Catholic participation inside the democratic process in Northern Ireland.

1966 TO 1969

Despite all the feuds and grievances that lay dormant under the surface, it was not until June 1966 that the first serious disorders began to occur in Northern Ireland. On 28 June Captain O'Neill announced to the House at Stormont that he had banned an extreme Protestant movement called the Ulster Volunteer Force, which he said was prepared to use murder as a political weapon. His statement followed two murders in the streets of Belfast on 27 May and 26 June, in which both victims were Roman Catholics; one was stabbed, the other shot. In addition, a seventy-year-old widow, who had been severely injured in a petrol bomb incident several weeks earlier, died on 27 June. There had been some instances of the bombing of Catholic churches and retaliation raids in Belfast from February onwards, which leaders of both Churches had condemned. On 28 June eight men appeared in court on charges arising out of these incidents. One of them was alleged to have told the police, 'I am terribly sorry about this, I am ashamed of myself. I am sorry I ever heard tell of that man Paisley, or decided to follow him.' There can be little doubt that some of the increased tension in the community was caused by the actions of the Reverend Ian Paisley, who had been campaigning against Captain O'Neill and his Government on the grounds that it was seeking conciliation between Catholics and Protestants. In more common language, Paisley was raising the old cry of the Unionist Government being soft on Catholicism; O'Neill had certainly been making conciliatory moves towards the Catholic community inside Ulster.

Paisley thus emerged as one of the foremost leaders of the reactionary movement, seeking to reverse the changes which Captain O'Neill was planning. In fact Paisley had taken a fundamentalist position for some years back. He repeatedly claimed that his organisation, The Ulster Defence Committee, sought to achieve its ends by peaceful and constitutional means only. Certainly, following the outlawing of the Ulster Volunteer Force, Paisley disassociated himself completely from it and said he knew nothing of either its leaders or its aims, but at the same time he repeated his call that O'Neill must go. At that time the call fell on empty ground; the Unionist Party was still united in its support of Captain O'Neill, as was the Orange Order which, at the Annual Assembly on 12 July 1966, condemned Paisley's call for O'Neill's resignation. It was not until later that the conflict was to cause splits in the Order and the Unionist Party.

It was not long before Paisley was to re-emerge, this time in the role of martyr. On 18 July he and six others appeared at Belfast Magistrates Court on charges of unlawful assembly outside the building where the General Assembly of the Presbyterian Church of Ireland was meeting. He and two of his closest supporters, the Rev. John Wiley and the Rev. Ian Foster, refused to enter bail or give assurances of good behaviour and so were arrested on the 20th and taken to Belfast Jail. On the day of his trial he was followed to court by a crowd of 2000 cheering Protestants, and on the day of his arrest he gave a public address entitled 'Why I chose jail'. He said he was going to jail to focus attention on the activities of the present Government, alleging that there was one law for what he called 'O'Neillites and Papists' and another for 'People who protest against Romanist tendencies in a Protestant country'. That his actions were rapidly polarising and intensifying the conflict was confirmed shortly afterwards by the Government's on all processions and public meetings within a radius of fifteen miles from Belfast City Hall for a period of three months. The ban also applied to gatherings of more than three people if they were likely in the opinion of the police 'to cause a breach of the peace or public disorder'. The ban followed serious disorders during the weekend of 23–24 July when the police fought running battles with Paisleyite supporters and teenage gangs, and there were numerous acts of vandalism, looting and window-smashing leading to many arrests. The trouble started when a procession of 2000 wearing Orange regalia attempted to march to the prison where Paisley was held; they were restrained by the police with a water cannon and later baton-charged after they attempted to raid a mineral wagon. By that evening a crowd of 4000 Protestants was marching around the City Hall chanting Paisley's name. For the following two nights the police broke up various mobs and forty arrests were made.

These riots and demonstrations raised fears for the visit of the Queen on 3 and 4 July. However, the visit was successful and large crowds turned up to cheer her. There were only two small incidents involving the throwing of a concrete block and a bottle, which the police did not consider political but merely the work of hooligans.

By this time the evidence was beginning to appear of increased British Labour Party and Government interest in the Ulster situation. On 5 August Captain O'Neill and his secretary, Harold Black, had a meeting with Harold Wilson and Roy Jenkins, then Home Secretary, at 10 Downing Street. Afterwards they refused to divulge the content of their talks, but Captain O'Neill did admit that they had discussed Paisley as well as the likely effects of the economic squeeze on Northern Ireland. This was also beginning to cause concern inside the Unionist Party, which contained people who felt outside interference in Ulster's affairs to be undesirable.

By October 1966 it became clear that opposition to Captain O'Neill's leadership had built up in the Unionist Party, many of whose members were alarmed at the liberalising elements O'Neill was bringing into intercommunal relationships. As well as making conciliatory moves towards the South, he was pressing for the introduction of a points system in housing allocation, an increase in house construction in Londonderry, and the establishment of machinery for investigating grievances in local government. Captain O'Neill announced that he had discovered on 23 April that there was a conspiracy against him after he returned from holiday. This crisis started with the signing of a petition by twelve members of the Unionist Parliamentary Party, calling for the resignation of the Prime Minister and criticising the Government's granting permission for the celebration in Northern Ireland of the fiftieth anniversary of the Easter Rising in Dublin. It also contained criticism of the handling of civil disorders and of a decision of the Ministry of Development which had aroused farmers. Captain O'Neill said that he was going to fight for the principle which he and the population knew to be the only way forward to a sound future, and that he was not going to give in to the Paisleyites. At a conference in Belfast on 24 April he was given a spontaneous vote of confidence by some 200 Unionist delegates. The back bench revolt ended on 27 April when he had a long question and answer session with the Parliamentary Party after which he received a personal vote of confidence closely followed by a vote of confidence from the Unionist members of the Senate. However, the crisis was also notable for the rather ambivalent support given to Captain O'Neill by his Deputy Prime Minister, Mr Faulkner, who had said on the evening of the 23rd that there was 'pretty strong discontent' in the Unionist Party, adding that he himself had 'steered completely clear of all such matters' and had refused to become involved in every kind of move. He had no comment to make on the leadership question 'at this present juncture'. It was later officially explained that Mr Faulkner had asked to be relieved of his duties as leader of the House in the view of the pressure of his departmental work as Minister of Commerce. He would retain the latter post and remain Deputy Prime Minister as hitherto; Major James Chichester-Clark would retain overall responsibility for the Whip's Office. However, as

O'Neill revealed later, he felt that his Deputy Prime Minister should have done more than steer clear of moves against the leadership inside the Party, and should rather have made clear his support for the Prime Minister.

The next major crisis indicative of trends inside the Unionist Party occurred on 26 April 1967 when Captain O'Neill dismissed from his Cabinet the Minister of Agriculture, Harry West, after the latter had refused to resign. The Prime Minister accused West of dealing in land and Government contracts in such a manner as to infringe the Code of Conduct for Ministers he had laid down in 1963. West denied any illegal or dishonourable dealings and implied that the Prime Minister and the Attorney General had conspired against him. The uproar which this dismissal caused owed something of its ferocity to some of the deeper divisions which had been appearing in the Unionist Party. On 27 April the Constituency Association of the Fermanagh Unionist Party, which covered West's constituency, gave him a full vote of confidence and also passed a vote 'of no confidence at all in the present Prime Minister of Northern Ireland'.

All this provided the backdrop to the sequence of events leading up to the situation in March 1969. It started on 13 June 1968 with what has become known as the 'Caledon Affair'.

Caledon is a mainly Protestant village in Dungannon Rural District. Under the usual system, the local Unionist Council had effective responsibility for allocating council houses in the area. Austin Currie, an MP, had encouraged squatting in two houses by two Catholic families who had come from another area where the Unionist Council had opposed the building of houses for Catholics.

Currie's particular complaint was that one of these houses had been allocated to a nineteen-year-old Protestant girl who was a secretary to the local Councillor's solicitor. He felt this to be blatant discrimination in view of the fact that there was a Catholic waiting list for houses in the area. The Councillor's explanation was that the girl was going to give accommodation to her own family and was also getting married shortly.

In a pattern which typifies the Northern Ireland situation, Currie raised the matter at all official levels from the local council up to the Stormont, where he received no satisfaction. Finally, with two of his friends, he formally occupied the house until, with great publicity, he was evicted by the police. (It is also typical that the policeman who evicted him was the brother of the secretary who was to take the house.)

This affair set off its own chain reaction. The incident aroused much latent antagonism against the housing policy in the area; this was further reinforced by the Campaign for Social Justice which had shown, in the results of a study, the strong discriminatory patterns of housing allocation. Currie persuaded members of this group to organise a march from Coalisland to Dungannon. Through Dr McCluskey, a member of the Campaign for Social Justice, the recently formed Northern Ireland Civil Rights Association was persuaded to agree to march on 24 August. Once again the response to this set the pattern that was to become familiar in the coming months.

Even though the police raised no objection in principle to the route the march was to take, Senator Stuart and John Taylor (respectively Chairman of the Urban District Council and MP for the area), both Unionists, declared Market Square, the destination of the march, to be Unionist territory and proposed the re-routing of the march. At the same time, many of those who were concerned with organising the march were threatened. It could thus be argued that the actions of the local authorities gave at least tacit support to the threats. In addition to this local action, the extreme Ulster Protestant Volunteers advertised a public meeting in the Square on the evening of 24 August. This action was a well-known tactic in Northern Ireland; by announcing a counter demonstration, the opposition forces the police into recognising a dangerous situation and calling off both meetings or processions. Thus the object of sabotaging the other side's march is achieved.

In the event, the march was rerouted and on 24 August the Civil Rights march was halted at a police barricade where fairly moderate speeches were made by the organisers. The demonstration passed off peacefully and was offered as proof of the efficacy of non-violent demonstration. On the other hand it significantly raised the expectations of other protest groups in Londonderry. The demonstration also caused considerable affront to some Unionists, in the light of police statements that many of the participants were Republicans and that some ten of the stewards were thought to be members of the Irish Republican Army.

After the Dungannon march the Derry Housing Action Committee started to organise a civil rights march in Londonderry. The group had already arranged some 'sit-ins' in token demonstrations which had received little publicity. This time they invited the Northern Ireland Civil Rights Association into the organisation of the demonstration. The Civil Rights group felt that the organising should be conducted by a more broadly based body and accordingly the Londonderry Labour Party, the Londonderry Labour Party Young Socialists, the Derry Housing Action Committee, the Derry City Republican Club and the James Connolly Society were brought in. These bodies were identified with strongly left wing and Republican attitudes and in some cases the membership overlapped. The organisation fell chiefly on the Derry Housing Action Committee, led by Eamonn McCann.

The planned route of the march broke with past convention in that it went through some traditionally Protestant areas. It had always been recognised in the past that different sectarian marches remained in their own areas. The justification given for breaking with this convention was that the Civil Rights group wished to demonstrate itself as being non-sectarian and willing to include all the deprived sections of the community, both Protestant and Catholic.

This was regarded with both scepticism and alarm by the Protestant community. By breaking with convention, it seemed to the Protestants that the Catholics were making a serious challenge to the existing political and social order, as in fact they were. There were objections to the march from the local Unionist headquarters and threats of counter demonstrations by the Middle Liberties Young Unionist Association and the Apprentice Boys of Derry. The latter claimed that Civil Rights was only a cover for a party of the Republican and Nationalist movements and they served notice of a procession to celebrate the 'Annual Initiation Ceremony'. The route of the proposed procession would cross that of the other marchers. The fact that such a procession had never taken place before again gave rise to some scepticism about its claim to be an annual event.

The local police duly informed the Ministry of Home Affairs that the proposed procession was dangerous, and all demonstrations in the city were accordingly banned by the Minister, William Craig. There was considerable debate among the organisers of the march as to whether or not it should proceed in defiance of the Government ban. After a series of informal and disorganised meetings it was decided to go ahead. It is argued in the Cameron Report that the organisers of the march were mistrusted by a large part of the local Catholic community and that they would have received little or no following had it not been for the ban. The ban increased the support for the march and attracted the presence of full press coverage and three British MPs. On the afternoon of 5 October a crowd gathered outside the Waterside Railway Station, the starting point of the march.

The police again claimed that members of the IRA were present as well as a large group of Young Socialists. Also present

was Mr McAteer, the Leader of the Opposition, some members of
the Nationalist Party, the Northern Ireland Labour Party and the
Liberal Party. More significantly for the future in Londonderry
there was also present John Hume, who had been active in organising a Credit Union and Housing Association in the City, and
had been prominent in the agitation for the establishment of a
second university there. Another individual who was to become
prominent in Londonderry was Ivan Cooper, a Protestant member
of the Londonderry Labour Party, who had been involved in
organising the march but whose tactics were wholly non-violent.

As our analysis given later will show, the groups present were
there for different and mixed motives. The police, not unnaturally,
expected trouble and brought in 130 men including two platoons
of riot police as well as two water wagons. The County Inspector
met the group outside the railway station and read out the
Minister's order, after which the crowd set off up Duke Street led
by Messrs McAteer, Currie and Fitt. The road had not been
blocked by the police because they did not expect the march to go
that way. A reserve force platoon was quickly moved to the head
of Duke Street to block the march and the water wagons were
stationed at the bottom of Duke Street, thus bottling in the
marchers, who when they reached the head of the street were
clubbed by some policemen who had had no orders to draw their
batons; both Fitt and McAteer sustained injuries.

At this point there was great confusion, but the crowd was
quieted by the stewards and some of the prominent people made
speeches. Those given by Currie and McCann could be interpreted
as more or less guarded encouragement to the use of violence to
break the police barrier. After about half an hour the meeting was
ended by Mr Sinclair, who requested those present to disperse.

What happened next was to change the whole course of the
protest movement in Northern Ireland. Some young people who
were members of the Young Socialist Alliance, most of whom
came from Belfast, threw their placards, banners and some stones
at the police. The police drew their batons and the County
Inspector ordered them to disperse the crowd. The crowd
retreated down Duke Street. The police at the other end had no
orders to let the marchers through and accordingly attacked those
coming towards them. Back at the top of the street the water
cannon were brought into action. The crowd was thus trapped
and subjected to indiscriminate violence by the police.

They eventually managed to disperse, but there was sporadic
fighting in the Bogside area of the town later in the afternoon.
Interestingly enough, there were some attempts to erect barricades

in the town at this time. There was a good deal of looting during the next day, before the police were eventually able to restore order. Eighteen policemen were injured and seventy-seven civilians were treated in hospital. It should be pointed out, however, that not all civilians would report to hostpital for fear of having their names taken down and reported to the police.

All these events received widespread coverage in the press and violence as a form of behaviour began to be normalised. Various groups were encouraged by these events to organise themselves for further protest.

October the 5th 1968 has very quickly passed into the mythology of both sides. By now the story has been inflated beyond its real proportions, but it is true to say that the lines of battle were drawn in Ulster on that day.

One immediate result of the events of 5 October was to give the protest movement a strong foothold in Queen's University, Belfast. Many of the students who had just returned to University were shocked by the events that had just passed and several demonstrations were arranged. The first was a march to Craig's house where he publicly, with full television coverage, accused them of being 'silly, bloody fools'. After this there was a meeting in the University where about 700 students decided to march in the city, dangerously near to the Protestant area, on 8 October. Their destination was to be the City Hall. On the day, Paisley arranged for nearly 1000 of his supporters to assemble round the Hall. The day ended in stalemate and the students returned to the University after a sitdown. They were by this time in a militant mood and the opportunity was afforded to Farrell and McCann, both members of the Young Socialist Alliance and former students at Queen's, to arrange for large-scale support. Another march was arranged to the City Hall on 12 October and it was during this time that the Peoples' Democracy was formed in the University by the more activist elements in the Civil Rights Movement. They organised more marches and sent groups, which frequently attracted violence, out to the county town to arrange discussions and demonstrations.

In the meantime, John Hume and other moderates in Londonderry had set up a committee of sixteen people called the Derry Citizens Action Committee. Their intention was to stabilise the situation and make use of more moderate methods of protest. McCann declined to take part, his opinion being that the new committee was middle-aged, middle-class and middle of the road. There was then a series of sitdowns and relatively peaceful marches. On 9 November Paisley and Major Bunting also staged a march which passed off without violence. The situation was kept under control and the moderates' position was reinforced by the Government announcement on 22 November outlining a reform programme. After Captain O'Neill's broadcast on 9 November the Action Committee called for a halt to demonstrations for a month.

On 23 November and 4 December there were clashes in Dungannon between Peoples' Democracy groups, followers of Major Bunting and the police. These incidents involved some arrests and stone-throwing. Another serious incident occurred in Armagh on 30 November. There, as in many other places, the events in Londonderry had inspired the formation of a local Civil Rights committee, which now decided on a march through the town. At once there were protests from local Orange and Unionist leaders, and the Ulster Constitution Defence Committee began to post signs in shops and other public places calling on all loyal Protestants to prevent Armagh from becoming another London-derry. Major Bunting proposed 'a trooping of colour and caval-cade' in the town. In the light of this, the police decided to reroute both marches and attempt to maintain a police presence between them. Despite the fact that the police erected road blocks round the city in order to search cars for firearms, Paisley and Bunting were able, early in the day, to gain control of the centre of the town with 1500 of their supporters. It is likely that some of them were armed because the next day the Armagh police announced that nearly 200 potential weapons, including daggers, bill-hooks and scythes, had been confiscated from cars. In the middle of the afternoon the marchers, now numbering over 6000, reached the town. The police were able to keep the two groups apart and the rest of the day was spent in stalemate, with a certain amount of stone-throwing until the crowds dispersed in the late evening. Five persons were arrested in connection with the possession of firearms, and a sixth man was charged with causing grievous bodily harm.

In view of the amount of weaponry and the hostile dispositions of the two groups, the injuries were relatively few—only twelve citizens and eight policemen were detained in hospital, mostly for minor injuries. The unpopularity of the Royal Ulster Constabulary with some of the demonstrators also leads one to believe that the low level of violence cannot be attributed solely to police control. The point is worth discussing because low levels of injury had been a persistent feature of the Ulster conflict. From observations made elsewhere by witnesses,[3] it would seem that the typical crowd situation involved two lines of demon-strators with the police either in the middle or just in front of the

Protestants. The two groups usually maintain a distance between each other of about twenty-five yards and the conflict is usually limited to throwing stones and the exchange of abuse. The situation only becomes dangerous for an individual if he breaks ranks, which, in the circumstances, he is hardly likely to do. As stones and other missiles are not very effective antipersonnel weapons the injury rate can be kept low. The conflict can thus be waged fiercely, but primarily in symbolic terms. This sort of confrontation thus differed greatly from the more widespread pattern of individuals being beaten up by groups from the opposing side, where the injuries sustained by the victim were likely to be more severe. The large confrontations throughout the winter and spring of 1968/69 were usually limited to the extent and duration of the announced processions or marches. Both sides thus would give notice of battle and give their opponents time to prepare for it.

The reaction of the Armagh Civil Rights Committee to the events of 30 October was to blame the Government and the police for failing to give them adequate protection from Ian Paisley's supporters. They issued a press release which stated: 'The obvious rights of the marchers on this occasion were clearly denied; while the police, whose duty it was to protect them, were not given the numbers to do so.' They also took credit for the non-violence of their supporters.

The first official reaction to this came from the Government five days later when Craig, the Minister for Home Affairs, increased the strength of the Royal Ulster Constabulary by two special platoons—the 'B' Specials whom the Civil Rights supporters perceived as being violently anti-Catholic. Thus, at least as far as the Civil Rights supporters were concerned, the Government's response was repressive.

During the preceding months Craig had established himself in the eyes of the Civil Rights Movement as a reactionary force. On 22 November 1968 he had declared in a speech that the Civil Rights Movement was bogus and consisted only of ill-informed radicals and Republicans. In the same speech he had expressed only qualified support for the creation of an Ombudsman, one of the reforms announced by the Government that day.

On 9 December, nine days after the confrontation in Armagh, the Prime Minister made a television broadcast in which he appealed for a swift end to the growing civil disorder throughout Ulster, and asked for the militant minorities to give his proposed reforms a chance to work. He further stressed the value of the political and economic link with Great Britain, and went on to say that Westminster could not be expected to continue giving aid if the reforms were not carried through. He then stated, in answer

to an argument that had gained some credence in Unionist circles:
'This paper is from Edward Heath and it tells me that a reversal of
the policies which I have tried so hard to pursue would be every
bit as unacceptable to the Conservative Party.' The Prime
Minister lastly reiterated that the Government could not tolerate
the breakdown of law and order.

This speech was interesting in that it emphasised the dilemma of
Ulster politics in being unable to satisfy anyone. First, although it
was somewhat more conciliatory towards the Civil Righters than
Craig's speech, it did not contain any reference to 'one man one
vote'. This issue had now gained much symbolic importance and
so long as the Unionist Government denied it they could not
creditably establish themselves as a progressive Government in
the eyes of the Civil Rights supporters. This point was probably
not lost on Captain O'Neill, but for the time being it seemed that
he could not get his Cabinet and party to advance. His call for a
return to law and order appeared to the Civil Rights people as a
threat as long as Craig was in charge of the police. So the stick
was perceived to be too big and the carrot scarcely credible to the
Civil Righters. However, the Conservatives in the Unionist Party
saw it the other way round; a promise of reform represented
appeasement, and the stick had not been effectively used.

That this division in the Unionist Party existed up to Cabinet
level became clear when Craig was dismissed from the Cabinet
two days after the Prime Minister's speech. The letters that these
two men exchanged are both interesting and informative.

In his letter to Craig, the Prime Minister stated: 'I have known
for some time that you were attracted by ideas of a UDI nature.'
He went on to reassert the value of the links with Great Britain
which were rapidly becoming the stalking-horse of Ulster
politics. 'Northern Ireland's Constitution is not in danger, for
both Parties at Westminster are committed to the guarantee we
have been given, but what is at risk are the numerous financial
subventions which make it possible for us to enjoy a British,
rather than an Irish, standard of living.'

Craig's letter in reply further demonstrated the extent to which
the links with Britain were becoming a rubric under which the
whole of the reforming issue was being debated. He stated that
Ulster was forced to depend on Westminster and claimed that
this was storing up problems for the future, predicting difficulties
when Britain began to shift to a system of more indirect taxation.
He came closer to the point when he rejected the idea that the
provision of financial aid gave Westminster the right to dictate
reform to Ulster. 'There has never been any cause to suggest that

Northern Ireland has used its powers improperly in the past, present or in the future. If Mr Wilson or anyone else should threaten to interfere in the exercising of our proper jurisdiction it is your [the Prime Minister's] duty and that of other Unionists to resist.' The point being made was that the Government should be allowed to deal with the civil unrest in any way it thought fit without outside interference. Craig had already made clear what he meant by this. As we have said, the disagreement between these two men typified the split in the Unionist Party. In the Cabinet the Prime Minister had been using the British connection as a counter for urging a conciliatory attitude on to his Government as well as the rest of his party and the country. His opponents maintained that the financial agreements with Westminster were never meant to convey extra political control beyond that made out in Article 75 of the Ulster Constitution.

The arguments used by the Prime Minister's opponents were subtle. They maintained that they did in fact support progressive policies but went on to say that they could not support Captain O'Neill as Prime Minister because he was too weak and gave in too easily to pressure both from Westminster and the Civil Righters. They thus never made open opposition to progressive policies—the line of attack at that time; they only maintained that reform in the face of pressure was an indication of weakness that could have serious political consequences. The greater the protests in the country, the more confirmed they were in this attitude.

So the battle had to be waged at all levels of the Party. After a long debate a vote of confidence in Captain O'Neill was passed at a meeting of the Unionist Parliamentary Party on 12 December. The motion gave him a personal guarantee of full support and was carried unanimously. There were, though, three significant abstentions. The individuals were Desmond Boal and John McQuade, both representing Belfast constituencies, and Harry West from Enniskillen, the former Minister of Agriculture who had been dismissed by Captain O'Neill in 1967. Craig and Thomas Lyons left before the end of the meeting. There was thus a core of tacitly declared opposition to the Prime Minister.

For the moment it had no support. A second resolution reaffirmed the Party's determination to preserve Northern Ireland's Constitutional position in the United Kingdom and repudiated any desire for UDI, a passage aimed specifically at Craig. According to press reports, by 13 December over 110,000 people had signed messages of support for Captain O'Neill. But no number of Unionist Party resolutions could solve the problem in Ulster, and the situation outside Parliament remained the same.

On 20 December, a week after the Unionist Parliamentary Party Conference, the leaders of the People's Democracy in Belfast announced that between 1 and 4 January they were going to march with their supporters from Belfast to Londonderry, via Antrim, Randalstown, Toomebridge, Maghera, Dungiven, Feeny and Claudy. The statement issued by the People's Democracy, along with the announcement, expressed dissatisfaction with the Government reform proposals of 22 November, and declared that the marchers would demand implementation of 'one-man-one-vote' in local elections, the total repeal of the Special Powers Act, and a 'radical re-thinking of the solutions of the problems of unemployment and housing'. The new Minister for Home Affairs, Captain Long, decided not to ban the meeting despite public warnings from a senior officer in the R.U.C. that Paisley's followers would be out in force. The Loyal Citizens of Ulster issued a statement calling on their supporters to harass the march and announced that Major Bunting would lead a 'trooping of the colours' in Claudy on 2 and 3 January.

On 1 January 1969 eighty marchers left Belfast. Their first confrontation with the extreme Protestants was on the bridge over the railway that leads into Antrim. The police set up a cordon between the two groups and there was deadlock for three hours until the marchers agreed to take police transport to their destination. The next day the march had to be rerouted three times to avoid ambushes, and the night had to be spent outside Randalstown. Meanwhile in Maghera that night a mob of 500 Protestants smashed up the town and had to be restrained by 200 policemen. There were four injuries in this incident. The march did not go into Maghera.

On the second day about 1000 people had joined the march, but had dwindled to 250 by the time they reached Burntollet Bridge on the way in to Londonderry. They were ambushed by extreme Protestants in the valley by Burntollet Bridge. The police agreed to take the marchers through the mob, but in the attempt fifty people were injured and had to be taken to hospital. After one more skirmish, the march reached Londonderry.

In Londonderry the marchers were welcomed by Ivan Cooper and John Hume, respectively Chairman and Vice-Chairman of the Citizens Action Committee. In Londonderry there had been violence from the night of the 3rd onwards. On that night Paisley and Bunting were addressing a gathering of their followers in the Guildhall. About 1000 Civil Rights supporters, mostly teenagers, gathered outside the hall and started throwing stones and bottles and trying to turn Bunting's car upside down. The police stepped in with water cannon and about thirty of the demonstrators sustained minor injuries.

There was more fighting between Protestants and Civil Rights supporters after a public meeting of the People's Democracy on the 4th, and sporadic violence carried on until the night of the 5th. In all, 126 people including twenty policemen were taken to hospital, and eleven people, including two policemen, were detained.

On the morning of the 5th, it was claimed at a meeting of about 2000 Civil Rights supporters that in the early hours of that day, a force of the Royal Ulster Constabulary had systematically terrorised the predominantly Catholic Bogside area, stoning windows in Wellington Street and St Columb's Well. Cooper, Hume and Fitt went to the Lecky police station and obtained assurances that the police would not re-enter the Bogside area in strength unless there was rioting there. The Civil Rights Society then organised about 1500 of their supporters to patrol the area with steel bars, hockey sticks and wooden clubs to ensure that no person should enter or leave. These patrols continued until the night of the 11th. It is important to note then that the Bogside area of Londonderry was virtually taken over by the Civil Rights Society and the People's Democracy for a week.

It was this fact perhaps more than any other that increased the pressure on Captain O'Neill from inside his own party to regain control of the situation. The fact that the town was occupied could not be avoided. Captain Long said on 6 January: 'Clearly there comes a point when agitation is not just expressing a legitimate point of view, but is attempting to bypass and discredit the ordinary processes of democratic government.'

On 5 January Captain O'Neill made a public statement that was terser in tone than that of December after the incidents in Armagh. He said, 'Two things have happened. Some of the marchers, and those who supported them in Londonderry itself, have shown themselves to be mere hooligans, ready to attack the police and others, and at various places people have attempted to take the law into their own hands in efforts to impede the march. These efforts included disgraceful violence, offered indiscriminately also to the police who were attempting to protect them.

'Had this march been treated with silent contempt and been allowed to proceed peaceably, the entire affair would have made little mark, and no further damage of any sort would have been done to the people of Ulster.

'It must be realised that in the whole of Ulster the regular police force amounts to only three thousand men; that is, one to each five hundred of the population. At times, one-sixth of the entire police force was guarding the march to Derry.'

He ended by appealing to those who desired civil rights to try to exercise civic responsibility.

The Londonderry Citizens Action Committee rejected the last point which they saw as an attack on themselves. They had, they said, exercised extreme restraint in the face of extreme provocation, and they would stick to their legitimate demands.

On the following day, 6 January, the Royal Ulster Constabulary was reinforced by greater use of 'B' Specials. The Ministry of Home Affairs announced on the 7th that an additional seventy members of the Special Constabulary would be mobilised for full-time duty with the Royal Ulster Constabulary, bringing the numbers called up on this basis since December 1968 to 175.

By this time pressure for further action was building up on O'Neill from within both his Cabinet and party, and it was increased by the next round of violence.

On 11 January a Civil Rights march into Newry ended in violence and the burning of police tenders after the police had banned part of the route. The march had been called by the Newry branch of the People's Democracy led by a man called O'Hanlon. He said when announcing the march that it was to be in support of the People's Democracy in Derry, and would be routed through the residential areas of both communities. The basic concern of the march would be to support the People's Democracy proposals for the right of free assembly and free speech, the ending of discrimination in housing and employment, the implementation of 'one-man-one-vote' in local elections, and the repeal of the Special Powers Act.

This announcement had been made on the 9th, and on the 10th a special Cabinet meeting was called to which Anthony Peacocke, then Inspector-General Designate of the Royal Ulster Constabulary, was invited. A statement was issued after the meeting to the effect that since there were grounds for believing that 'the procession over a portion of the proposed route may occasion a breach of the peace or public disorder', an order had been made under the Public Order Act rerouting the march and reducing its total length by about 600 yards. The People's Democracy in Newry issued a statement saying that in doing this the Cabinet had succumbed to pressure from the right wing.

Major Bunting gave orders to the inhabitants of Newry to draw down their shutters and stay at home, in order to 'place the responsibility for the maintenance of law and order firmly and squarely on to the shoulders of the government.' This turned out to be a

good move for the extremist Protestants, for the events of the
next days were to strengthen considerably the hand of the conservatives in Party and Cabinet.

At the point of the change of route, 5000 marchers confronted
100 policemen in front of two lines of crash barriers and police
tenders. At this confrontation, most of the marchers went home.
A group of about 100 remained against the barriers all evening
and eventually attacked the police tenders, pushing one in the
canal, and setting three on fire. All the fighting seemed to be
between police and civil righters. Eighteen civilians and ten
policemen were injured, and there were twenty-four arrests.

There were two immediate responses from the Government to
all this. First, Captain Long accused the Newry branch of the
People's Democracy of carrying out a brutal attack on the police.
They replied that the police action was an incitement to violence,
and that despite that fact the vast majority of marchers had left
when asked to do so.

Second, on 15 January the Stormont Government announced
the calling of a high level independent commission of inquiry into
the unrest in Ulster. At the same time new measures were
announced that strengthened the laws of procession and increased
many penalties for disturbance.

These measures were duly seen by the Civil Rights supporters
as more evidence of oppressive government. Their version of
events was rather different. 'The awesome show of police strength
was nothing less than incitement to violence of people who were
determined to be peaceful. It was a sad and lamentable thing that
some gave way to a provocation which might well have been
calculated so as to discredit the Civil Rights movement . . . the
great majority of marchers dispersed when asked to do so by the
committees and the marshals. What followed at the barricades
and later elsewhere in the town were sad events caused mostly by
young people excited and frustrated by the continued blockade of
the town by police.'

Eddie McAteer, the Nationalist Party leader, greeted the commission of inquiry as a belated move in the right direction. It was
met with fury by the more right-wing sections of the Unionist
Party. It was thought that the commission, which was to be
headed by Lord Cameron, would end by recommending one-
man-one-vote, which Captain O'Neill could then say he felt obliged
to legislate for, against the stated policy of the Unionist Party. The
more sophisticated among them took the line that Captain O'Neill
should decide with the Cabinet what ought or ought not to be
done, and then take it to the Party, rather than delegate the

decisions to someone else. Mr Faulkner, the Minister of Commerce, gave in his resignation on these grounds, as did William Morgan, the Minister of Health and Social Services. Until then Faulkner had been Deputy Leader, so the defection was an important one. The letters they exchanged showed the deep divisions in the Cabinet, and also the resentment that O'Neill felt at not having his Cabinet's full support for his reform policies. It was also evident from the letters that the commission was the Prime Minister's idea.

O'Neill's position was thus severely weakened, with the departure of another able opponent from the Cabinet. On 30 January, two weeks after the proposal to institute a commission, thirteen Unionist back-benchers wrote to the Secretary of the Unionist Party Organisation asking for a meeting of the Parliamentary Party to discuss a change of leader. The signatories were Boal, McQuade, Hinds, West, Craig, Lyons, Burns (who resigned that day as Assistant Chief Whip), Hawthorne (a former Chief Whip), Anderson, Captain Ardill, Brooke, Dobson and Taylor. Hawthorne later withdrew, claiming that he did not fully realise what he was signing. Their letter stated that: 'being convinced that the disunity in the Parliamentary and in the constituency associations had reached grave proportions, and being dedicated to the principle that the progressive policies of the Unionist Party must be vigorously pursued by a united party, we are satisfied that there must be a change of leader.'

On 31 January the Government responded with a declaration of full support for Captain O'Neill, as did the Ulster Unionist Party. Evidently the dissatisfaction had not gone far enough for the official party machine to change its allegiance. The meeting of the Parliamentary Party was not held. On the morning of 3 February the rebellious back-benchers held a meeting in Portadown, although owing to the withdrawal of Hawthorne, and the absence of two others, there were only ten people present.

After the meeting, the following statement was released: 'We have no dispute or disagreement with the current policies of the Government . . . the Unionist Party, under the leadership of Captain Terence O'Neill, has seen a steady decline in the unity of the party each year of his administration, now reaching its zenith. Undoubtedly, the serious rioting provoked by the march of the People's Democracy from Belfast to Derry and the ensuing anarchy in the city of Derry for more than a week, without any effort made to re-establish the rule of law, also undermines the credibility of Captain O'Neill's government. It is manifestly clear that the Government, by appointing a commission at the time it did, made it inevitable that it would be compelled to implement the findings of the commission. . . . To summarise: (1) We want unity; (2) we want stable government; (3) we want firm leadership and Cabinet government; (4) we want realistic progressive policies for all.'

The Government reacted by saying that they had been prepared to hold a Parliamentary Party meeting on the 5th, and that in meeting in Portadown the rebels' 'action was inconsistent with honourable standards of political conduct. The Prime Minister had therefore decided to dissolve the House and call a general election.'

By appealing directly to the electorate the Prime Minister was trying to some extent to circumvent his opponents nearer at hand. In the meantime, the machinery with which to implement reform was being constructed. On 30 January the members of the Londonderry development commission were announced. The leader was B. Morton, a member of Belfast City Council; members included S. McGonagle, Secretary of the Londonderry branch of the Transport and General Workers Union, and seven others, mainly businessmen from the Londonderry area.

It is difficult to see what an election could have decided: most of the rebels had safe seats so the electorate had already safeguarded the rebellion; only if O'Neill were to suffer defeat might the Party take a big swing to the right. In the event, he came uncomfortably close to being unseated by the Rev. Ian Paisley.

The general election, held on 24 February, resulted in the return of the Unionist Party with a majority of twenty seats over all other parties and groups. The election was notable for the large number of constituencies contested by the various opposition groups, and the division in the Unionist Party, reflected at the polls, between supporters and opponents of Captain O'Neill's leadership.

Of the thirty-seven Unionist candidates officially adopted by local constituency associations, twenty-two were regarded as supporters of Captain O'Neill, thirteen as opposed to his leadership, and two as uncommitted, while the Independent Unionists comprised fifteen supporters of Captain O'Neill, most standing against official anti-O'Neill candidates, and three opponents fighting official supporters of Captain O'Neill.

Of the thirteen original signatories of the letter of 30 January opposing O'Neill's leadership, nine, including West, Craig and Burns, were re-elected as was Faulkner. In fact, outside Belfast, the independent O'Neill Unionists, except in Larne and North Derry, largely failed to erode the traditional Unionist vote, and in four constituencies, including those of Faulkner and West, they came bottom of the poll. The Protestant Unionists on the other hand, while not actually gaining any seats, made a substantial showing at the polls, as did the People's Democracy.

In a comment on the results O'Neil said: 'In the battle for moderation, obviously these things are going to take time to achieve. Maybe we cannot achieve them all at once. It is also apparent from the figures that this has worked better in urban and suburban areas than in the countryside where things change slowly.'

On 28 February Captain O'Neill was re-elected Prime Minister by a vote of twenty-three to one (Craig), with one abstention (Faulkner)—ten members having previously withdrawn from the meeting. The ten comprised eight of the original signatories plus two new members, Dr Laird and Mr Mitchell, from St Anne's and North Armagh. The ten members then issued the following statements: 'In view of the failure of the Prime Minister to justify his flagrant breach of party loyalty by openly canvassing support for independent candidates, we felt that his actions must be considered by the Standing Committee of the Unionist Party, and their views ascertained, before we could responsibly consider his adequacy as leader of the Parliamentary Party. Our request for an adjournment of the meeting was rejected by the die-hard supporters of Captain O'Neill, who did not appear to attach much importance to the opinions of the Standing Committee.'

The situation then was very much the same as before the election, and the vote of confidence in the Prime Minister that was finally elicited from the Standing Committee on 7 March could only be described as qualified in view of the voting of 183 to 116 in favour of his leadership.

On 31 March, after a hard-fought meeting of the Unionist Council, the Prime Minister received his third successive vote of confidence by 338 votes to 263. In a speech at that meeting he said that Northern Ireland should have representatives who would be listened to at Westminster, and emphasised that the Party had never been stronger, and that people even crossed sectarian lines to vote for it. 'We should take this historic opportunity to renew and strengthen the whole fabric of Unionism.'

The Queen's speech was read out on 4 March; it announced Bills to establish an Ombudsman and to amend the Public Order Act; and a Draft Order for the assumption by the Londonderry Development Commission for the administration of and full responsibility for the area covered by the Londonderry Area Plan. It was also stated that the Government was actively pursuing consultations with local authorities for the adoption of schemes for the equitable allocation of houses. The appointment of Sir

Edmund Compton as Ombudsman and new members of the
Cameron Commission were also announced.

A reminder of the communal situation came with two further
events. First, nine opposition members were suspended from the
House after sitting on the floor and singing 'We shall overcome'
after a substantive and procedural disagreement over the Public
Order Act, and Paisley and Bunting went to gaol for three months
for their part in the earlier disturbances.

SUMMARY

Several points are apparent when we view the development of the
conflict. It is not reasonable to distribute praise and blame, for it
is apparent that the actors were operating rationally inside their
own sets of perceptions. It is also apparent that a crisis moves one
very quickly into a situation where real communication breaks
down and actions speak louder than words. Each response is the
basis of the other party's next move, and if one thing is certain it
is that both sides will misinterpret each other. It is also clear that
the dominant side cannot make reforms quickly enough. A spiral
of rising expectations starts on the oppressed side and the reforms
never catch up with the expectations. While this is happening,
political control becomes more diffuse, local groupings can set
the pace which they are able to do because violence becomes the
least ambiguous communicator. Anyone with a petrol bomb can
spur any town into action. Meanwhile the established parties tend
to start splitting up, as is seen by the rifts in the Unionist Party.
One should also point out that in such a situation the role of a
third party is extremely difficult.

We have traced the patterns of interaction and the path to
violence in Ulster. In doing this we have stepped in a rather
cavalier fashion over a great many assumptions. Our next task,
therefore, is to look carefully at the theory of intercommunal
conflict and intervention in order to gain a more rigorous understanding of Ulster.

[1] For a good background in the history and structure of the conflict see
D. P. Barritt and C. F. Carter, *The Northern Ireland Problem,* Oxford University
Press, 1962. More recent work includes the Cameron Report, *Disturbances in
Northern Ireland,* Cmnd 532, H.M.S.O., 1970.

[2] Anders Boserup, *Power in a Post-Colonial Setting,* Institute for Peace and
Conflict Research, Copenhagen, 1969.

[3] J. C. R. Bayley and Peter Loizos, 'Bogside off its knees', *New Society,*
21 August 1969.

[4] Figures taken from D. P. Barritt and C. F. Carter, *op. cit.*

3

The theory of intercommunal conflict

CONFLICT THEORY AS APPLIED TO INTERCOMMUNAL CONFLICT

We are now in a position to try to relate some of conflict theory to a real situation. There are three ways in which this can be done. The first type of application of theory is the analysis of a particular type of situation in the real world. For example, we may see what conflict theory has to say about intercommunal conflict in general—the procedure in the first section of this chapter. It is to be hoped that it will provide us with a framework of analysis and draw attention to certain basic underlying features which are universal to this type of conflict. Such a procedure, however, fails to account for the unique elements in any particular situation.

This is where the second type of analysis becomes relevant. In this the same general principles of conflict theory are applied to a particular specific situation. In our first example Robin Jenkins[1] measured the extent of polarisation and prejudice in five communities in Northern Ireland and related his measurements to the population balance between the two communities in those areas. Analysis of this kind performs two functions. First, each tested hypothesis adds to the body of our more general knowledge about conflict. Second, such analysis identifies the major problem areas and central actors in a given social situation. Thus Boserup[2] draws our attention to some major structural features in society, such as the decreasingly powerful position of the traditional élites, and Jenkins provides us with some supporting evidence for Boserup's analysis by locating and identifying the 'marginal man' in Northern Ireland—those people who create social change by straddling the conflict boundary.

Such analysis takes us only so far. Because the propositions tested relate to the broad outlines of a society, they cannot relate to the day-to-day and place-to-place features of any particular conflict. For example, Boserup's type of analysis can identify seven parties as being the major actors in a situation and give a broad outline of the relationships between them, but it could not predict the week-to-week or month-to-month train of these relationships because of the complexity of the theorising involved. Here we are at the level of microdynamics. The theory of detailed conflict dynamics is seriously underdeveloped and this third area is considered in Chapter 5. It should be emphasised that these three different levels of analysis are cumulative: one cannot start work on stage three until stages one and two have been undertaken.

A MODEL OF INTERCOMMUNAL CONFLICT

Our model starts with the simple proposition that the size and nature of the social groups in which a person chooses to live are determined by several relevant considerations, *which may change* according to circumstances. The considerations may be such things as the degree of participation that a person feels he has in the decisions that govern his way of life, or the reference group that a person chooses to regulate his behaviour. Thus Biafrans, Scottish, Welsh and Irish nationalists and Turkish Cypriots, amongst others, argue that their previous membership of a large political unit is now unsatisfactory for them, and that they should have greater control over, and participation in, decisions that affect their area. To this end they may argue that their present membership in this unit is a result of powerful domination by another group, or that the circumstances in which they obtained membership of that unit are no longer relevant.

The general point is that the values they now hold make the past state of affairs unacceptable to them. They may or may not be correct in their calculation of the material and social gains and losses involved; but such considerations will be subordinate to their perceptions of the situation. A look at the current thought on the subject of nationalism helps to develop this reasoning. Kelman, for example, argues that it is possible to regard nationalism as a system of ideas and attitudes: 'The ultimate justification for maintaining, strengthening, or establishing a political system with jurisdiction over a particular population is that this system is most naturally and reflectively representative of that population, it is this feature that provides legitimacy and cohesiveness of the nation state.'[3]

Thus boundary changes will have a greater significance to the group concerned in that they will fundamentally affect the degree of control they have over their environment and the relations they have with neighbouring communities. And the urgency of the need for a reflective boundary can be easily conveyed within the group because it is just that ease of communication that made them a group in the first place.

This argument throws light on several different conditions involving some kind of geographical or social separation of different groups in the same country. Here one could mention a Cypriot situation where a minority group feels that its interests are not reflected by the political regime and therefore demands separation. On the other hand it also explains a violent reaction against partition when partition represents a move away from a reflective political system. The example of postwar South Korea illustrates this.

However, we have not yet fully explained these two possible reactions. We can only say that we have explained them when we have some way of predicting where and when different groups are going to want to change their boundaries and the nature of their relations with other communities. So far we have stated nothing that would prevent one from expecting that the Post Office Tower may soon declare UDI. In order to gain this predictive ability we would have to know the level of frustration and the nature of the demands being made, and also understand the political dynamics of the group. We return to these problems in Chapter 6, but first we must deal with another line of argument.

The first step of the argument here was to look at the composition of complete countries and see on what lines they could come apart. We could turn this argument on its head, and think about how separate social groupings could be brought together. There is a large body of literature concerned with social integration and we can use some of the ideas contained in it. The literature points to the importance of structural prerequisites, such as interlocking and interpenetrating economic systems, and behavioural and attitudinal prerequisites, such as the possession of common goals and political styles. Geographical proximity is also obviously regarded as being important.

These ideas are relevant to our consideration of divisions in a society. Areas that have been partitioned from outside and countries that are divided by the existence of one or more socio-cultural boundaries could be reckoned to have at least as good if not a better chance of reintegrating than separate national states. Such areas should fulfil all the necessary characteristics, mentioned above. It is perhaps this sort of thinking that allows many people to accept the idea that Germany will be eventually reunified—it is after all 'the same country'.

However, most partition and intercommunal conflict situations tend to maintain themselves for relatively long periods of time once they have started, and are often characterised by all the features of a completely polarised conflict. Korea is an example; all communication between the two sectors goes through the United Nations mission at Panmunjon, and this relationship has remained fairly constant for the last fifteen years or more.

The relative permanence of such divisions must lead us back into a reconsideration of integration theory. In a recent monograph a well known political scientist used a model based on five different indicators of integration: (1) social and cultural homogeneity; (2) political attitudes and external behaviour; (3) political interdependence; (4) economic interdependence; (5) geographical proximity. [4] Now it is worth noting that the first two categories are quite often absent in intercommunal situations. However, the other three are just as likely to be present and so it is worth enquiring why they do not act more powerfully as integrating forces. One of the monograph's findings is that pairs of states linked together by these sets of factors are twice as likely to fight as other pairs of states. This is relevant to civil strife as well. The reason for that research finding was that the indicators used are in themselves indicative of nothing more than interdependence and salience. That is to say before two areas can become integrated they have to interact with each other and be relevant to each other. These same conditions apply to conflict between different entities. One could therefore identify two entities as being responsive to each other and susceptible to the effects of each other's actions, but we have as yet no guarantee which way that susceptibility will run.

Let us use as a simple model the notion of two communities that are both interdependent and salient to each other. Now, let us postulate one hostile move, or a move that is perceived by the other side as hostile. In such a situation, the *interdependence* on both sides will be felt as *vulnerability*. It is dangerous to be dependent on a party who is not trustworthy. For a political leader the costs of not taking defensive action in such circumstances are potentially high. A situation is created where it is irrational for the leader to trust the other side. So the suspicious party must take defensive measures that look hostile to the other side, especially if, as is likely, they involve the withdrawing of certain benefits. To give an example of what may seem to be too abstract a process: after various intercommunal incidents during British rule in Cyprus, and wrangles at the independence conference, the two communities could not depend on each other to maintain the political *status quo*, so they both took the precaution of bringing

F

arms into the island. After a shooting incident in 1963 the leaders on both sides could hardly, with prudence, avoid mobilising their forces, a move which, while maybe precautionary, could only look offensive to the other side.

Thus some precipating cause may start a process which is the result of rational and logical actions by both sides, and the escalation may be started *whether or not there is any real conflict or intent on violence*. It should be emphasised that we are not saying that there is never any 'real' conflict or harmful intent, in fact there is almost certainly bound to be some on the part of some members of each side for reasons which we shall attempt to show later. The point is that at this stage of the analysis we have identified a process by which escalation can occur simply as a result of some visible division between people and prudent planning by their respective leaders.

It should be noted that these processes are by no means peculiar to conflict in divided countries, but are a special case of a more general phenomenon.

In such a situation the government or controlling body on either side of the line has four courses of action open to it. They could increase their autonomy by attempting to become more self-sufficient and make the border even harder. They could look elsewhere for the benefits they obtain from the other side, for example, divert more trade overseas. They could attack the other side in order to obtain the benefits of cooperation without cooperating. Lastly, they could attempt to win the cooperation of the other side. The dilemma of such situations is now even more apparent. The first two courses of action are more than likely to be interpreted as hostile by the other side; the third is openly hostile; and we have seen how difficult the last course of action is in such circumstances. It should also be pointed out that the first two courses are apt to increase the likelihood of outside intervention because of the need for outside aid.

So far then we have posited conditions which, given some precipitating factors, can cause two groups of people who are separated by some social dividing line to become involved in an escalating conflict.

Despite any hostility that may be involved in the situation this escalation can theoretically stem from opposed value systems, arguments over the allocation of social rewards (such as money or political position), or any other such elements. We also note that such conflicts will face the parties concerned with a set of options that will radically affect their structure and their future interaction with each other and, possibly, with third parties.

We must now relax some of the assumptions made earlier and introduce some of the factors mentioned in Chapter 2.

VALUE SYSTEMS AND THEIR EFFECT ON PERCEPTION

In order to maintain commitment and mobilisation in any community, it is generally agreed by sociologists that some element of myth is needed. It will be based on the past history of the group and will be emphasised in times of stress and change as an indication of commitment to the basic values of the group. 'The myth must be judged as a means of acting on the present; any attempt to discuss how far it can be taken literally as future history is devoid of sense. It is a complex of remote goals, tense moral moods, and expectations of apocalyptic success.'[5] It is our initial contention that in the conditions of social and political conflict that we have hypothesised, myth becomes involved with political demands as a way of maintaining commitment to them, and very quickly obscures the original source of conflict. Thus in Cyprus and Northern Ireland both sides cling strongly to myths about their own future which are devoid of present political practicality (Enosis, Orange and Hibernian ideals), but which inflate their own demands in the conflict and serve to reinforce the picture that the other group has of them. An example is the fighting in Ireland in August 1969, started by a ritual march of the Apprentice Boys of Derry.

The danger is that such myths tend to rely heavily on a hostile picture of the outside world, if only by virtue of asserting the rightful supremacy of the group that holds them, and can be transmitted into action through the mechanism of the self-fulfilling prophecy. 'The self-fulfilling prophecy is, in the beginning, a false definition of the situation evoking a new behaviour which makes the original false conception come true. . . . The specious validity of the self-fulfilling prophecy perpetuates a reign of error.'[6] The point is that myths, no matter how untrue, do have very real consequences; that prophecies based on initially false perceptions can produce conditions which really exist and thus fulfil the prophecy; that men react to symbols by real action. 'If men define situations as real, they are real in their consequences.'[5] What is immediately apparent is the way in which this can support and indeed propel the sort of rational process of escalation that we pointed to earlier. It is as though this escalation process can draw in feedback from the cultural system to support it—amplifying feedback. And this is not surprising when we bear in mind another point we made earlier, namely that conflicts over boundaries and jurisdiction of a group have fundamental importance for the cohesion and survival of that group.

There is another phenomenon closely associated with the self-fulfilling prophecy—the dissonance effect.[7] Having attributed certain characteristics to the out-group, all new information about the out-group will be fitted into the prescribed pattern, and any information that is highly dissonant (incongruous) with original conceptions is suppressed or ignored. In the self-fulfilling prophecy the other party is led to behave as he was originally perceived; in the dissonance case he will be perceived in conformity with the image held of him, regardless of his actual behaviour and any information that may exist about him. For example, a de-escalation on the part of the enemy will be attributed not to goodwill or a desire to terminate the conflict, but rather to trickery or a desire to play for time. The reception of Captain O'Neill's reform programmes in Ulster by his opponents during the course of his premiership is a good example of this.

At a more 'psychological' level, there are significant gains in reduction of ambiguity from naming as enemy a party whose actions are unpredictable. Such a definition immediately indicates what attitudes and behaviour to adopt and relieves one of the necessity to indulge in complicated, time-consuming learning behaviour. Thus both processes, self-fulfilling prophecy and dissonance, when linked with myth pictures of the world and prudent action by political leaders, combine to work in the same direction. But it is undoubtedly the irrational element which is the most escalatory—'Emotional commitment to a symbol is associated with contentment and quiescence regarding problems that would otherwise arouse concern.'[5]

One more point. The continued use of symbols satisfies the interest of those who desire what they think these symbols represent. They can only fulfil their unifying function among large groups if they are ambiguous and capable of wide interpretation. They are therefore unnegotiable. Their renunciation is likely to be one of the last concomitants of policy change—yet in symbolic conflicts, the demand is for the other side to give up its symbols or ideology. Robert Merton claims that a circle of self-fulfilling prophecy can be broken—'the initial definition of the situation which has set the circle in motion must be abandoned'.[6] But, as we have tried to show, this definition may be embedded in sets of symbols which are a part of the system-maintenance structure of the group concerned, and perhaps only susceptible of slow change.

None of what we have said so far is especially new, nor is any one part of it unique to intercommunal conflict. It is also over-emphasised, in that there are mechanisms that counteract some of the spiral processes we have indicated. The important point is to realise how these features combine with each other. This is one of the more important conclusions that begins to emerge—that *violent civil strife contains and combines almost all the arsenal of escalating mechanisms known to conflict research.* It is this fact that makes such problems so intractable and so potentially dangerous. This will become clearer as we relax the image of the dyad and deal with the two sides in such a conflict as being composed of many elements among whom different interests are distributed in different proportions, thus affecting their attitudes and behaviour. We will then be faced with a number of conflicts within the one conflict pursued by many different interests.

DIFFERENT INTERESTS

There are several concepts that may be used to relax the assumption that the two groups facing each other will be unitary. It is in fact a matter of common observation that such conflicts as we have been describing will be subdivided both across and within the two major parties.

It may be assumed that the values held by any group will be distributed throughout the group in some sort of normal curve, the bulk of the community being 'middle of the road', the leadership consequently being moderate, surrounded by extremes of harder and softer attitudes. It is plausible to hypothesise that in times of conflict or stress, when the values of a group appear to be under threat, more extreme and harder statements of core values will be forthcoming, and will be likely to find wider support than in normal times, just because the rest of the community feels some sort of threat. An interpretation of this sort could be applied for example to Powellism. The consequence of this would seem to be that a moderate leadership will of necessity be forced to harden its attitudes if it is to retain the main political ground available. This is to say that the government will have its hawks to placate. In so far as it accedes to hawkish demands, it is also likely to have doves on the other side urging softer attitudes. The interplay between such factions and the state of a conflict are by now well-observed phenomena, and are commonly used as indicators of the political state within the parties to a conflict.

The relevance of these phenomena has been even further established by recent work which indicates that those closer to the centre of a conflict will tend to see it in instrumental terms, if only because as leaders they are likely to have more interaction with the other side and are also able to empathise with the problems faced by the opposing leadership. Those further away from a conflict, in terms of interaction with opponents, are likely to see it in more value-orientated terms (better dead than red). This is likely to be even more pronounced in a traditional society where the bulk of the people are living in rural areas, where value systems always tend to be more conservative than in the towns. Where two such communities live together, or at least opposite each other, as do Greeks and Turkish Cypriots and Catholic and Protestant Ulstermen, the conflict at this level is likely to have a completely different emphasis and meaning.

The differences in value between the two major groups of the sort that we have indicated are likely to have wide implications in terms of everyday living. The ways in which these differences are rationalised and controlled at the town and village level makes for opposition of a different kind to that found at the political centre where broader considerations of political balance are likely to be considered. We thus have another level of conflict which is important if only because it seems able to function independently of the political centre, and probably requires different resolution techniques. For example, it is not always clear how much fighting between local Catholic and Orange mobs, or Turkish and Greek Cypriots, is under the control of the political centres of each side, and this can have a powerful escalating effect. The Greek Cypriot leadership maintained that in 1963 the attacks against the Turkish Cypriots were outside their control, that their attempts to stop it were unsuccessful. The other side were unimpressed by this, if only because in such cases the two sides tend to see each other as being more unitary than they really are, not having enough information to be able to differentiate between different groups on the other side.

There is one more general way in which the groups may be subdivided. This depends not on the value that particular sub-groups may hold, but on the interests they have. Groups which live on or near the boundary (geographical or social) will have stronger threat perceptions than those further away; and there may be groups who previously interacted across the boundary line who will have an interest in reopening it. In both Cyprus and

Northern Ireland there are pressure groups of businessmen from both communities who traded with one another before the two lines hardened and would like to see the conflict ended. There must also be other groups who for similar reasons have an interest in seeing the conflict perpetuated. The extent to which such groups will be a complicating factor will depend on their position in the political system. For example, in Cyprus a great deal of local conflict is transmitted into the political system by virtue of the status of many of the ex-EOKA leaders who command a great deal of local support. The same is probably true of the Orange Order in Ulster.

We thus have a picture of conflict that is intersected by different conflicts within and between the parties, on grounds of both value and interest.

THE CONSEQUENCE OF SIZE DISPARITY

At this point we return to the main model to add its fourth major element, size disparity. So far we have pointed out how the mere fact of proximity and interdependence between any social dyad raises the possibility of an escalation to violence between them merely on the basis of rational decisions taken by both parties. We then pointed out how the value structure of both sides, closely tied in with their conceptions of their boundary as a group, could feed into the initial spiral providing further grounds for violent opposition. With this in mind we pointed out, thirdly, how the distribution of values and interests within the groups forced us to relax our image of a dyad and think of two broad overarching communities containing different subgroups who would have different attitudes and behaviour towards the conflict between the two main groups and, consequently, different levels of amity or hostility towards other subgroups in the same main group. The implications of all this are fairly clear for negotiation and resolution, but we must consider two more main elements in the model before we discuss this.

In objective terms, the processes that we have examined do not provide a 'real' grievance over which it would seem rational to fight—that is, neither side could be said to have an overwhelming case. Indeed the processes belong to the 'automatic' variety. We have described two groups side by side, separated by almost any major relevant line one cares to name, and then detailed conditions under which they could find themselves at war. It also seems that a great deal of the conflict research literature is of this order—descriptions of how parties can find themselves in a state of violent conflict by virtue of misperceptions, escalating processes and the like. There is not a great deal of discussion of the actual issues that may be at stake, the assumption perhaps being that once all the misperceptions are cleared away, it is only a matter of attention to detail. However, at least in the sort of cases with which this model is concerned, it is apparent that the parties may not only *feel* discriminated against, but actually *are* discriminated against. One of the major causes of this, and of other effects, is the existence of a size discrepancy between the two parties.

Cases of violent conflict between communities of roughly the same size are rarer than those where there is equality. One may conceptualise a scale which extends from the point where one group vastly outnumbers the other to the point where the two sides are of an equal size. At the former point on the scale, one would expect the smaller group to be so negligible as to be invisible. For example, there are small communities of Armenians and Maronites in Cyprus, but they are politically invisible. At the other end of the scale, the two communities are of nearly or exactly equal size. Here one would expect a stalemate in power terms—or rather, both sides could credibly threaten each other in a roughly equal and reciprocal fashion. One would then expect relationships of either bargaining or stand-off (hostile or friendly), and would anticipate actual conflict in the absence of outside involvement to be limited, of short duration, or non-existent: the sort of relationship which has characterised the relations between East and West Germany in recent years.

Between these two extremes, where the mix is imbalanced (say from 80 : 20 to 60 : 40) one would expect the situation to be unstable. From the point of view of the majority community, the smaller side is 'powerful enough to threaten but not to deter', that is, they can appear as an irritant that could be crushed, given enough trouble. From the minority side, the superior size of the adversary provides a constant threat against which precautions must be taken, which in turn serve to increase the irritations of the bigger party. Thus one of the greater needs of the smaller side is simple security—some guarantee or barrier against attack. They cannot afford to rely on trust in the face of the potential threat. On the stronger side, the complaint is usually that the minority cannot be trusted to behave: if they would only stop being suspicious and give some token of their commitment to the system, then they could expect more tolerance. But this is something that the weaker can never afford to do, and a cyclical process can start. The stronger side makes concessions that are in its view substantial;

the weaker side is more suspicious and follows a policy of 'wait and see'. Inside the majority community the critics of appeasement gain strength as the policy is seen to produce no results. Pressure builds for 'firmer action' which reconfirms the opinion of the minority community of the aggressiveness of the larger one.

The reaction will be all the sharper if in the past the larger community has used its superior power to operate the political system to its advantage—that is to gain a monopoly of decision-taking over issues of 'national importance' and to insure preferment of its own members in as many social fields as possible. Here we end up firmly in the field of discrimination. In response to this it is also likely that, in any area where it has control, the smaller community will also discriminate. We are thus confronted with a set of issues that considerably complicate any resolution process. It is difficult to persuade a minority that their best long-term security lies in working for as open a relationship as possible with the other side: a situation that requires lowering their defences. One can imagine their reply.

It also raises a basic dilemma of politics which provides the underpinning of most of the issues of contention in such conflicts. It is whether democracy consists of the counting of heads, which gives the majority community control of decision-making processes within an area, or whether legitimacy depends on the effective transmission of the opinions of the relevant groups concerned in any decision with some chance of their being implemented and allowing for the possibility of a smaller group to have a veto at least over decisions which it regards as of fundamental importance to itself. This is of course too bald a statement of the dilemma and we will have to examine it more carefully when we come to consider negotiation and resolution. It does however appear to be a fair paraphrase of the dilemma phased in Ulster and Cyprus, as well as in other areas like Malaysia, Fiji, the West Indies, Vietnam, in fact in most areas where a population is divided into two unequal parts by some form of communications barrier.

OUTSIDE INTERFERENCE

The fifth and final element in the basic model may be introduced by the observation that many of the situations we have been discussing involved the presence of an external power or powers. We must be interested then in how far outside intervention can be an escalating factor in this sort of conflict, in the nature of the links between internal conflict and external involvement and in the likely effect of external involvement on internal conflict.

FACTORS SUSTAINING INTERVENTION

Work being done by C. R. Mitchell[8] and others suggest that, for the outside power, intervention has self-propelling characteristics. It is worth briefly enumerating these characteristics, because they will manifest themselves inside the 'target' area as a sort of constant outside 'push' once the outside power is intervening effectively.

(*a*) *Commitment of resources*. Once capital of any kind has been invested, it should be seen to produce results. For example, once an area has been secured militarily benefits in the form of security, control and, frequently, economic gain will be expected. If they are not forthcoming, often the only obvious solution is to spend more capital so that the first injection is not wasted; this may be described as 'good money after bad'.

(*b*) *Multiplier effect*. This refers to the process where perimeter defences come to be perceived as vital national interests, any erosion of which is the thin edge of the wedge. Thus further positions are taken up to defend this perimeter defence. The continual forward movement of the United States South-east Asia defence and containment line since the Second World War is an example.

(*c*) *National prestige*. This is closely connected with the last. Any external defence position may come to be a symbol of national prestige and power. The list of objections raised to the British evacuation from east of Suez contained many value-orientated references of this nature. If the position was established as a defence against an enemy, then any retreat from it is seen as a 'surrender', or 'loss of face'.

(*d*) *National solidarity*. This is in turn connected with national prestige. The possession of external positions may become a symbol of national solidarity. This leads to the more tendentious point that external positions may provide useful focal points for the public in times of internal crisis.

(*e*) *Defence planning*. If the outside power is a member of an alliance there may be pressure from other members to maintain perimeter positions as part of the alliance's overall defence. Again, the objections raised by the United States to the retreat from east of Suez provide us with an example.

Taking these points as given, we can proceed to an examination of the links between intervention and civil strife.

BOUNDARY-CROSSING SYSTEMS

We have already described the case of two communities becoming hostile towards each other. If the affective and cultural links that bind the two separate parties together stretch across the political boundaries of the state into other states, then other parties can become almost automatically a part of the conflict system. Thus Greece and Turkey feel themselves to be a part of the Cyprus conflicts and feel a certain commitment towards the wellbeing of their 'dependent' communities. In the same way, Catholic Ulstermen regard themselves effectively as a part of Eire, as Protestant Ulstermen feel themselves to be a part of Great Britain. These are in the nature of affective links; it may be that instrumental links can work the same way—that intervention can be made on the basis of pressure from groups with powerful economic or commercial interests in the wellbeing of a minority group. Or there may be a weak and indirect affective link—like the commitment to self-determination that bound French policy to Biafran goals. This leads one again to suspect that the cold war boundary lines drawn between East and West may not be purely a result of the relative strength of the two super-powers. This is particularly apparent from the nature of the guerrilla fighting that is waged around the periphery—it is easier to defend areas where one has had some previous interaction and where there will be some sympathy for one's cause. Obviously the introduction of new parties creates new fears and new conflicts. The whole problem is at once more complex.

We can leave the abstract model here. It should provide a satisfactory background for the analyses with which the second part of the chapter is concerned. The two chosen studies are both examples of the application of conflict theory, at a macro level, to a particular case, Ulster.

PREVIOUS RESEARCH

The first piece of research that we wish to study is that undertaken by Robin Jenkins and John MacRae in Ulster in 1966.[1] As they mention in the introduction to their report, this was the year when Ulster had first been drawn to the attention of British public opinion. As we saw in Chapter 2, in 1966 the Queen visited Ulster and her car was damaged by a stone, Ian Paisley was sent to jail, the Ulster Volunteer Force had come into being, Prime Minister O'Neill had met with the Premier of Eire, the Archbishop had visited the Pope in Rome and the Ulster Government had given the Catholics permission to hold processions commemorating the Easter Rising of 1916. Each of these events had caused considerable disquiet in one section or another of Ulster society and further trouble was expected that year although it did not materialise. Jenkins and MacRae described their project thus: 'Five towns were visited and 361 people were interviewed, using a closed ended questionnaire. Of these, 172 were Protestant and 189 were Catholic. In each town random samples were drawn from the Westminster Electoral Rolls. The total sample drawn was 524, making a return of 68 per cent.

Their intention was to verify how much polarisation there was in the different towns. They found that the more nearly equal were the two communities in any particular town, the more polarised was the social situation. They also found that the higher the level of polarisation, the less did the two sides indulge in normative institutional conflict. For example, the more polarisation there was in any particular town the greater was the prejudice held by both groups, the more likely it was that the Catholic population would abstain from voting and the fewer would be the number of contacts between the two communities. The tables shown below give some indication of their findings.

Religion and income[1]

	Protestant	Catholic
High income	45	31
Low income	48	60
DK and NA	8	9
Total	100	100

There is a significant departure from a random distribution in the table. With education there is a less striking relationship. However, even if religion is a dominant variable in explaining the social expectations of people in Northern Ireland, this does not necessarily mean that Northern Ireland is polarised. Wherever Protestants and Catholics live in the same area, their religion is able to account for income differences (Lenski 1961), the Catholics having a lower average income.

When it comes to interaction between Catholics and Protestants, a clearer pattern emerges. There is diffuse interaction over a whole number of dimensions (e.g. marriage) and specific interaction over few dimensions (e.g. buying bread). The data show that the more diffuse the interaction, the greater the number of negative bonds between the two groups.

Attitudes to specific and diffuse interaction (all towns)[1]

Type of interaction	mind	don't mind	DK NA	total
people you work with	9	89	2	100
people who live next door	41	58	1	100
people you marry	71	21	2	100

Religion and voting behaviour (all towns)[1]

	Protestant	Catholic
Unionist	81	2
Republican	1	31
Liberal	0	13
National Unity	0	4
not vote	18	40
Total	100	100

Segmental participation rests on social conflicts and the clearest thing that comes out of any study of Northern Ireland is that there is only one real conflict and because this is a conflict about values, it results in a polarisation rather than an active conflict which could be beneficial to the society.

The correlation between religion and voting behaviour really is striking. Unfortunately it is not possible to determine whether religion or politics is dominant, given the present data. However, it is clear that there is little segmental participation across the religious-political boundary and it is also clear that parliamentary politics is about values in Northern Ireland, not about norms as it is elsewhere.

Conflict and Polarisation[1]

Town	% Catholics in town	% Catholics not voting	Polarisation Index	% Catholics saying Protestants want too much power
Portadown	23	68	65	63
Kilkeel	43	21	59	62
Dungannon	53	34	60	80
Armagh	60	45	56	84
Newry	87	40	26	71

These results are hardly startling, but they are useful as confirmation of what one would expect. Jenkins and MacRae draw several conclusions from their study. The first is that different racial groups are more cohesive when they are polarised. They mention that it is easier to spread rumour within a polarised group because of the high level of consensus. The more polarised the system the easier it is for people like Paisley to spread fear-dominated propaganda. This supports the conclusion reached earlier in the book that it is easier for a polarised system to get worse rather than better. Jenkins also points out elsewhere that the greater the distance between two groups, the more likely it is that the masses in these groups will perceive the conflict in affective terms, that is they will think of the conflict as a black and white one rather than one concerned with the balancing of different interests. Those people who interact between the two communities (often those in leadership positions) are more likely to see it in instrumental terms, that is as a problem of resolving conflicts of interest.

When considering ways out of conflict the two researchers mention the importance of the marginal man, i.e. the person who by virtue of birth straddles the two communities. They give some evidence of the existence of such people and pinpoint their location.

Proportion of friends who are of opposite religion[1]

	about $\frac{1}{2}$	over $\frac{1}{2}$	nearly all	all
Catholics with Protestant friends	39	6	7	1
Protestant with Catholic friends	18	2	2	2

(Expressed as a $\frac{1}{2}$ of their own religious group)

These are the marginal men who are the key to change in Northern Ireland. . . .

It is very probable that the marginal men in Northern Ireland are either products of mixed marriages or are implicated by relation to mixed marriages. Certainly, the difference between them and the rest is most clear concerning opinions about marriage.

*Do you mind whether one of your family marries a
Protestant or a Catholic?*[1]

	Mind v. much	Mind not v. much	Not at all	DK
More than ½ friends of opposite religion	33	26	36	5
About ½ friends of opposite religion	42	27	27	3
Less than ½ friends of opposite religion	68	16	15	1

Opinions on co-operation and interaction produce a similar
pattern.

Opinions of marginal and ordinary men[1]

(Marginal man is here defined as one, more than ½ of whose
friends are of opposite religion to his own.)

	Unification of the Church		
	agree	disagree	DK
Marginal man	68	26	6
Ordinary man	68	40	12
	Meeting between Archbishop of Canterbury and the Pope		
	Approve	Disapprove	DK
Marginal man	85	10	5
Ordinary man	63	28	9
	Meeting between Capt. O'Neill and Mr Lemass			
	Approve	Disapprove	DK	Total
Marginal man	88	4	8	100
Ordinary man	70	21	9	100

The marginal man is the one most open to segmental
participation, but in Northern Ireland, marginality has not
reached over into politics in the five towns visited. There is
some indication, especially in Belfast, that the marginal
political parties (marginal in two senses—they cater for
marginal men and they are at present in the margin of
Northern Ireland politics)—Liberal and Labour—are attract-
ing increasing support from both sides of the polarisation
boundary.

Thus they are forced into an optimistic conclusion with regard to the role that could be played by such people. The second possible way out of the conflict that they could see is through the increasing secularisation of society.

Did your parents go to Church more frequently, less frequently or about as often as you do?[1]

	Protestants	Catholics
More frequently	42	29
About as often	45	64
Less frequently	11	6
DK and NA	3	1
Total	100	100

Would you say that you attend religious services more often, about the same, or less frequently than you did five years ago?

More often	18	9
About the same	52	82
Less frequently	29	7
Total — NA	100	100

Practice and belief are more closely related in the Catholic faith than in Protestantism (Lenski 1961). Thus it is unlikely that a Catholic will change his pattern of religious practice appreciably once adult, though significant differences occur between generations. The Protestants are losing their ties with the Church rather quicker, something which is to be expected because of the closer relationship between belief and practice.

But for men to identify with classes there must be class organisations and class consciousness. In fact, all the organisations most important to the growth of such a new focus of identification are already divided according to religion and this perpetuates religious identifications and boundaries. Trade Unions are as subject to religious differentiation as other organisations.

The work done by Jenkins and MacRae is therefore invaluable in revealing the exact nature and distribution of some of the processes at work in the society

The research work done by Anders Boserup[2] is of a different order. The technique that he uses is to apply conflict theory to a close historical analysis of the conflict in Ulster. He produces an argument which can be summed up in distinct stages. He first draws attention to the fact that the Government in Ulster has many characteristics which make it similar to a post-colonial government. Northern Ireland has many essentially English institutions, such as the major political and legal systems. It contains an élite markedly oriented towards the English style of life. Economically and politically Ulster is heavily dependent on Great Britain. British industries have formed the major growth sector in Ulster, while the traditional industries such as agriculture, textiles and shipbuilding are in decline. The Government and its associated élites, therefore, have nothing like complete political power, and the power they do possess is being rapidly eroded. In this view, the conflict between the two communities is an essential key to understanding the whole society, for it is the only way in which Unionist dominance can be maintained. The argument, therefore, states that the society and the conflicts it contains are structured in this way precisely because it is consciously or unconsciously in the interests of a defensive, élite group that it should stay this way. It is no coincidence that there is no class conflict in Northern Ireland. This is usually the case where strong ethnic conflict is found. It is true, for example, of Belgium as well. The whole social structure of Ulster would be changed drastically by class conflict; it therefore requires no great stretch of the imagination to regard the society as being structured precisely to prevent this eventuality. This solves the problem of why religion has obstinately refused to disappear as a key social force as it has elsewhere in Europe. Religion has survived because it performs a thoroughly secular social function.

Boserup supports this general thesis by broad analysis of the sequence of events leading up to the 1969 troubles. The first major protest group to march in the middle 1960s was the Campaign for Social Justice. This group was mainly composed of Catholic professional strata. They gained their relative wealth by virtue of the fact that some British firms in the growth sector were prepared not to discriminate between the religions. Their campaign was concerned mostly with middle-class aims and so not directly towards the mass of the catholic population (whom Boserup, in an earlier survey had found to be almost entirely apathetic at that time), but rather towards the general British public, and in particular the British Labour Government. This ties in with Jenkins's findings about the role of the disequilibriated man as a factor of change in such conflicts. These people

G

were to some extent separated from their own people by virtue of
wealth and profession, yet because of their religion were not
granted the professional and social amenities of the middle class
by the Protestant community. The fact that the mid-1960s saw the
arrival in power of a British Labour Government was another key
factor. Whether or not the Government actually put pressure on
Ulster for reform is a moot point, but Boserup argues that the
mere existence of a Labour Government was a source of increased
pressure for liberalisation in Ulster. Such pressure could only be
regarded as a threat by many members of the élite group. This is
where the phenomenon of frustration, induced by a sort of
ex-colonial helplessness, is relevant.

Those reforms that were forced out of the Ulster Government
caused strong Protestant reaction which came first from the
poorer sections of the Protestant community. This corresponds
with Galtung's theory. The Protestant poor are denied the social
power and wealth associated with the Protestant ascendancy, yet
feel themselves unable, by virtue of their religion, to unite with
the Catholic poor; rather, they use the Catholic poor as a scape-
goat for their own disequilibriation. Thus we see change being
forced by such groups on each side.

The speed of the consequent polarisation was surprising; to
quote Boserup: 'Consequently the mere rumour of reform would
create a reaction from the Protestant middle and working class in
the form of Paisleyism, a movement which, in the Spring of 1966,
had still appeared like the rumble of a distant drum. By the end of
1967 20 per cent of the Protestant middle class and almost 40 per
cent of the Protestant working class found that they "usually
agreed with what the Rev. Ian Paisley said".'

This again corresponds with Jenkins's remarks about the
quickly increasing ease of transmitting rumour and hostility
inside a highly polarised community.

Analyses like the two we have discussed allow us to apply
conflict theory to a close analysis of the whole or some part of a
particular conflict. Were the funds available a battery of such
surveys would enable Britain's decision-makers to take action on
the basis of a much greater understanding than they are likely to
have at the present moment. It is our contention, however, that
such analysis does not completely 'explain' a conflict. Having
identified the main conflicts and actors in a situation, one must
then proceed to examine each issue and actor in some detail and
work out all the possible interactions between them. It is the state
of interaction at this level that make up the day-to-day dynamics
of any conflict. If conflict resolution means the restructuring of a

society along lines of increased social justice, then one must have the necessary information to tackle the job. It is not enough to say merely that sectarianism supports a dislocated élite, we must be in a position to spell out all the consequences of alternative structures and also have sufficient knowledge to allow us to predict with some confidence how change introduced in Sector A will interact with Sector B to Z.

[1] R. Jenkins, *Conflict and Polarisation,* presented at the British Sociological Association 1968 Conference, Peace Research Centre, London (mimeographed); R. Jenkins and J. MacRae, *Religion, Conflict and Polarisation in Northern Ireland,* Peace Research Centre, Lancaster (mimeographed).

[2] Anders Boserup and Claus Inersen, *Papers of the Peace Research Society,* viii, 1967; Anders Boserup, *Power in a Post-Colonial Setting: the way and whither of religious confrontation in Ulster,* Institute for Peace and Conflict Research, Copenhagen (mimeographed).

[3] Herbert C. Kelman, 'Patterns of personal involvement in the national system: a social-psychological analysis of political legitimacy', in *International Politics and Foreign Policy: a Reader in Research Theory,* ed. J. N. Rosenham, Free Press of Glencoe; Collier-Macmillan, 1969.

[4] Bruce M. Russett, *International Regions and the International Systems: a Study in political ecology,* Rand McNally, 1967.

[5] Georges Sorœ, *Reflections on Violence,* New York, Collier Books, 1961.

[6] Robert K. Merton, *Social Theory and Social Structure,* rev. edn., Free Press, 1957.

[7] Leon Festinger, *Theory of Cognitive Dissonance,* Row, Peterson, 1957.

[8] C. R. Mitchell, *Civil Strife and the Involvement of External Parties,* C.A.C. (mimeographed).

4

Fieldwork

Though we wished to carry out an analysis of the conflict in Ulster, we were restricted by the terms and conditions of our grant to a study which involved a small research team and a limited period of actual fieldwork. This meant that it was impossible to undertake any large-scale study of the population. Within the smaller communities the one which appeared most worthy of study in terms of moving towards a better understanding of the conflict was that of the political leaders.

The actual study involved interviews with political leaders of all the parties to the conflict, using a prepared series of questions. The design covered a number of problem areas which this chapter discusses. The first concerns the necessity for interviewing decision-makers during rather than after a crisis, while the second asks what sort of interview design is most appropriate. The third involves the choice of question and the attendant problems of reliability and validity. The fourth area concerns the definition of the parties and political leaders who make up the dispute and how to draw up an interviewing sample from them. The fifth area covers the actual difficulties involved in designing and carrying out the interview studies in Ulster and Dublin. This leads to a discussion of the problems which arose in conducting the interviews, an analysis of their cost effectiveness, and an enquiry into why it was so easy to obtain access to political élites. The chapter finishes with a description of a subsequent visit paid to Ulster to observe the fighting in Londonderry in the autumn of 1969.

THE TIMING OF THE INTERVIEWS

There is nothing new in interviewing politicians. Political journalists spend much of their time seeking and being granted interviews with leaders before, during and after crises. Social scientists have been more reticent and have conducted such interviews only some time after the crisis has ended. These remarks apply to interviews for publication since many are granted which are strictly off the record. Our aim was to obtain enough interviews to make it impossible to ascribe any statement to a specific individual when the answers were combined.

From the viewpoint of the social scientist, the information a journalist normally reports after an interview with a national decision-maker is not analysical enough to be useful. A journalist's approach tends to be descriptive and prophetic, seeking to describe what is happening, and to predict who is likely to do what, rather than analytical and seeking to abstract processes common to similar situations in other conflicts. The situation in Ulster is rarely, if ever, compared with structurally similar conflicts in Cyprus, Belgium and Fiji. The other disadvantage of the journalistic approach is that the politician knows that he is going to be publicly quoted: he is thus limited, first by the image he wishes to project, secondly by his role as Government spokesman, and thirdly by the risk of exacerbating the conflict situation and/or any negotiations which are taking place. This could happen if, for example, he appeared to be adopting a more flexible position than the Government. A further danger is that the politician may in fact be using the journalist to send a message to a party or a country, bypassing more formal channels of communication which may either have broken down or become temporarily blocked. An example of this in British politics is the unattributable cabinet leak.[1] A difficulty here is that the person trying to interpret the politician's comments may not be aware of their communicating function.

For the social scientist there are numerous disadvantages in interviewing political leaders weeks, months or even years after a particular crisis. As time passes people remember specific details of events less and less accurately and those which remain tend to be those which are congruent with the overall picture of that particular decision.

Bartlett's classic work[2] on rumour shows not only that some events are forgotten, but also that others become distorted, and yet others may be invented to present a total recollection. One explanation of how this comes about is given by Festinger's work on cognitive dissonance theory, where it is argued that in order to reduce the anxiety about whether one has made a correct decision, there is a tendency for the individual to seek out cognitive events which justify a particular decision, and to ignore or repress those which run counter to it.[3]

A further disadvantage, and another reason for distortion, is given in Goffman's work on the presentation of the self, which indicates that people control their behaviour so as to present as favourable a picture of themselves as possible. [4] They are therefore unlikely to admit events which run contrary either to the image they have of themselves or to that which they wish to present to others. A good example of this was the series of television interviews in which President Johnson looked back on his period of office. Most commentators on the American scene agreed that his recollection of events gave a distorted version of what actually occurred.

Another disadvantage of *post hoc* interviewing is that in a time of crisis there is likely to be emotional tension which may affect the rationale behind any decision taken. When a person is interviewed some months or even years after the event, it is probable that this emotional segment of the decision-making process will will be forgotten and only the distorted cognitive aspects will appear. A final disadvantage of this approach is that it becomes virtually impossible for there to be any cross-sectional comparison between the perceptions of opposing factions. This is because even if all parties can be interviewed at some subsequent date, any comparison of their answers will be a comparison of numerous distorted, barely recalled versions of what they thought occurred at the time. Only if all the parties to a dispute are interviewed within a reasonably short period can a valid comparison be made.

The obvious answer to the set of problems raised above is for social scientists to interview political leaders while crisis decisions are being made. This was what we set out to do in Ulster, even though we were warned:

1. that we would not be granted access. To this we replied, 'If journalists, why not us?' setting the answers, 'Because journalists can be useful to politicians but you can't';
2. that we would not be told the truth;
3. that we risked physical injury. To support this we were told a gruesome story of how the last person to interview one of the right-wing Ulster extremists had left two teeth on his living-room floor.

The reasons why we think we were granted access will be discussed later in the chapter.

INTERVIEW DESIGN

At the initial stage of the project we carried out an analsisy of available data. This was, first, to draw up a background picture of the conflict; secondly, to aid in the identification of parties; finally, as a tool in the selection of political leaders. Theoretically, once this background analysis had been completed it would have been possible to take a number of speeches of political leaders about similar issues, carry out a content analysis and thus compare how people from opposing sides saw the same issues. There were many good reasons for not adopting this approach. The first of these was a lack of comparable data for each of the political leaders. The problem was that while the speeches of Cabinet ministers and leaders of opposition parties were freely reported, those of second-rank political leaders were not. Thus there was a difference in the relevant amount of data available. Secondly, speeches were rarely reported in full, and edited versions might have been biased for or against a particular group, depending on the political interests of the organ of the mass media concerned. Thirdly, even though two speeches might be about the same issue, they might have been given for different purposes.

An alternative would have been to use mail questionnaires: we could have sent a series of standardised questions to the chosen sample of political leaders. Again, there were cogent arguments against this. First, the chances of a high proportion of the questionnaires being returned were slight as there would have been little chance to establish sufficient rapport to give them priority in politicians' overloaded intrays; therfore, even if answers had been received, it is probable that they would have been only a synoptic version of what might have been obtained from an interview. Secondly, in the less structured opposition parties, part of the sampling of the political leaders, as discussed below, was done by chain sampling, technique in which each interviewee is asked to recommend further possible sample members. This would not have been possible with questionnaires or a data analysis approach. Thirdly, the use of questionnaires would have prevented any probing, either on answers which appeared to be incomplete or on those which gave the appearance of opening up new insights into the situation. To design a questionnaire comprehensive enough to cover these contingencies called for a longer acquaintance with the problem area than was possible. Finally, postal questionnaires raise considerable problems of reliability and validity. It is not possible to ascertain who completes the questionnaire and whether all are answered with the same degree of seriousness and veracity.

It was therefore decided to use interviews. They are flexible, both in terms of who should be interviewed and the range and complexity of the questions that can be asked; they enable rapport to be built up with the subject; and in a study such as this it is easier to check through interviews for the reliability and validity of answers.

There are a number of different interviewing techniques we could have used. At one extreme there is a depth-type, completely unstructured approach with no specific questions but simply general areas for the interviewer to cover. This encourages the subject to talk as much and as freely as possible and is useful for obtaining underlying beliefs and motivations; its disadvantage is that the areas to be covered and the level at which they have to be considered are so vague that it is difficult to categorise answers and thus compare responses.

At the other end of the range of possible approaches is the highly structured interview with a preponderance of closed questions. Closed questions, which restrict the range of possible answers to those given by the interviewers, require extensive piloting, and this would have needed more time and money than was available. Because of their design, they limit the complexity and depth of any answers and in a situation as nebulous as Ulster this could have provided too biased a picture.

The final interviewing form chosen was that described by Merton and Kendall[5] as a focused interview whose characteristics are:

1. Persons interviewed are known to have been involved in a particular concrete situation . . .
2. The hypothetically significant elements, patterns and total structure of the situation have been previously analysed by the investigator. Through this 'content analysis' he has arrived at a set of hypotheses concerning the meaning and effects of determinate aspects of the situation.
3. On the basis of this analysis the investigator has fashioned an 'interview guide' setting forth the major areas of enquiry and the hypotheses which locate the pertinence of data to be obtained in the interview.
4. The interview itself is focused on the 'subjective experiences' of persons exposed to the pre-analysed situation. The array of their reported responses to this situation enables the investigator to:
   (a) test the validity of hypotheses derived from content analysis and social psychological theory; and
   (b) to ascertain unanticipated responses to the situation, thus giving rise to fresh hypotheses.

From our study of the hypotheses we were interested in we fashioned an interview guide concentrated on the subject's perception of the situation. This guide was a structured interview with twelve open-ended questions. It was felt necessary to put the same questions to all subjects to ensure comparability of answers and the questions were open-ended to cover as wide a range of opinion as possible within the area covered by each.

One inadequacy of this approach is that conflicts are dynamic and not static; what is of interest at any one stage is not necessarily so at any other. For example, the potential invasion by Eire of the North which was a distinct possibility in August 1969 was not as immediately relevant an issue as the internal conflict within Ulster in January 1969. Thus a study which focuses an any one time interval in a conflict is likely to exclude information which could be of vital analytical concern later.

CHOICE OF QUESTIONS

The twelve questions:

1. As regards the political situation, what would you like to see happen in Ulster in the next three months?
2. Now speaking realistically, what do you actually expect will happen in Ulster in the next three months?
3. Now considering the next five years, what developments, if any, would you like to see happen?
4. Again, speaking realistically, what do you think will happen in Ulster over the next five years?
5. Given what you would like to see happen in Ulster in the future, what do you think are the most effective ways to achieve these aims?
6. Taking each of these ways in turn, do you think there is any danger in using any of them?
7. Could you briefly indicate what you think are the critical points in Ulster's history which have led to the present situation?
8. Which groups or countries outside Ulster do you think might interfere in Ulster's politics, and why?
9. Could you please describe what you think are the most important problems that Ulster has to solve at the moment?
10. How do you think each of these problems is going to be solved?
11. Which people or forces in Ulster do you think might prevent

these problems being solved? What motives or reasons would
they have, and what tactics might they use?

12. How would you describe each of the different groups of
people which play an important part in Ulster's present
problems?

The questions were aimed at providing general insights into
the processes of intercommunal conflict. Part of the design of
the questions came from hypotheses about perceptions in crisis.
These hypotheses have been brought together by Jenkins[6] and
those relevant to the study are listed in Appendix.[4] In addition,
from our own knowledge of the situation we expected at the
outset to find differences in perceptions towards the conflict
between: (a) opposing religious groups; (b) those inside Stormont
versus those outside; (c) those with legitimate power to alter the
situation versus other grouping.[5] As the study progressed we
changed our approach and adopted a more flexible system of
classifying parties. This greatly increased the number of groups
between whom differences would be expected in terms of their
answers to the questions.

SELECTION OF POLITICAL LEADERS

The first problem was the identification of parties to the dispute.
At this stage we still worked within the conventional approach
of identifying parties by their historical and institutional labels,
though later this proved to be theoretically unsound (see Chapter
5). A variety of approaches were used at this stage:

1. Stormont elections of February 1969—this identified the
parties who participated in the political system by putting
forward candidates, namely:

Official Unionist
Northern Ireland Labour
Republican Labour
National Democratic
Protestant Unionist
People's Democracy
Liberal
Nationalist
People's Progressive

Other candidates stood as Independents, Independent O'Neill
Unionists and Unofficial Unionists.

2. In addition a content analysis was carried out of *Keesing's Archives* and the *Belfast Telegraph* for the period January to March 1969. This indicated that other political groupings less directly concerned with parliamentary representation played a part in determining events. These included the Orange Order, the Civil Rights Association, the Press, religious bodies, and a number of intercommunal parties with mixed religious membership.

On closer examination it became possible to divide the parties into four groups:

Pro-O'Neill Unionists, including many official Unionists and all candidates who stood as Independent O'Neill Unionists;
Anti-O'Neill Unionists, including official Unionists, Protestant Unionists and Unofficial Unionists.
Established Opposition, including the Northern Ireland Labour Party, Republican Labour Party, the Nationalists and successful Independent candidates, (i.e. people who worked primarily through Parliament);
Civil Rights/People's Democracy, i.e. people who influenced events outside of Parliament.

There are a number of points to make about these groupings :

(*a*) Smaller parties with no successful candidates were included only when they appeared to exert an observable influence on events in Ulster. Therefore parties such as the Liberals were excluded while the Protestant Unionists were taken into consideration.
(*b*) At this stage we were primarily concerned only with parties inside Ulster. In an intercommunal conflict this is an artificial boundary to draw but it was at the time dictated by the costs of the project. Later it became possible to include the parties in Eire actively concerned with events in the Six Counties of the North.
(*c*) Many groupings had overlapping memberships. This was particularly true of the Established Opposition and Civil Rights/People's Democracy groupings when some of the Opposition candidates were also members of the Civil Rights Association. Which group an individual belonged to was decided by the extent to which he appeared to work through official parliamentary parties or through extra-parliamentary processes. As it turned out, when we moved away to a more flexible categorisation of parties, this no longer remained a problem.
(*d*) Of the parties which did not put up parliamentary candidates we decided to include only the Civil Rights Association and the

intercommunal parties. The CRA was included as with the
People's Democracy, it had been instrumental in setting off the
whole protest movement which had led to the present crisis.
The intercommunal parties were included to serve as a control
group for the others. It was contended that the other parties
could be said to hold opposing views on what they wanted to
see happen in Ulster, and how this should be achieved, and that
members of the intercommunal party, being by definition moderates, would hopefully present a middle of the road view.* The
Orange Order was excluded for two reasons; firstly, with only
one known exception, all the Unionist M.P.s were members of
the Orange Order and therefore its influence and opinions would
indirectly be ascertained through interviewing the MPs; and
secondly because being a closed society it would probably have
been more difficult to penetrate. The press was left out because
the success of the study required a complete absence of publicity
and if we talked to the press there was always the danger of a
leak. The lack of publicity was necessary to ensure confidentiality
of the respondents and their answers. Finally, we decided to leave
out the religious parties, not because they were not influential,
but because we wanted to concentrate on the leading political
decision-makers and the religious leaders appeared to exert
only an indirect influence at this level.

The next stage was to draw up a list of the sample of political
leaders in each of the five groupings:

(a) *Pro-O'Neill Unionist.* It was possible to identify which of the
Unionist M.P.s were for O'Neill and which against by three
methods: first, by an analysis of candidates standing for the
February election because in many classes Unionists representing
different factions contested the same seat; second, by a study of
events in Stormont over the previous months, where various
crisis meetings had clearly indicated which MPs supported
O'Neill's policies; finally, by an anlysis of the reported speeches
of various MPs. As there were a total of thirty-nine Unionist

* For example, the constitution of PACE has as its aims:
(a) to promote harmony and goodwill between the religious and political
communities in Northern Ireland;
(b) to demonstrate that, although people may be separated by differences of
conviction, there are many activities in which they can freely unite in
order to work together for the common good of all;
(c) to work with all who desire the establishment of a social order based
upon justice and charity, and enlivened by mutual respect and understanding, thus leading to the elimination of the factors which produce
harmful divisions in our society.

MPs of whom twenty-five were pro-O'Neill, it was decided to restrict the parliamentary sample to successful candidates only. We also included senior positions in the Unionist Party administration in this sample.

(*b*) *Anti-O'Neill Unionists*. By the above methods, it was possible to identify fourteen out of the thirty-nine Unionists as being against O'Neill. The elections were also useful in identifying leaders of the smaller anti-O'Neill parties as four Protestant Unionists and one Ulster Unionist stood unsuccessfully as candidates. Again, a content analysis of the *Belfast Telegraph* assisted in identifying right-wing extra-parliamentary leaders.

(*c*) *Established Opposition*. As there were only ten successful Opposition candidates in the election (excluding three Independents), it was decided to include unsuccessful candidates standing for the Nationalist, Republican Labour and Northern Ireland Labour Parties, (i.e. those parties who had at least one MP) and this raised the total number of candidates, successful or otherwise, to thirty. Also included in the sample were the senior party administrators in each of the Opposition parties.

(*d*) *Civil Rights/People's Democracy*. This was the hardest grouping in which to define a sample of political leaders. In fact the People's Democracy claimed that it had no leaders. However, in the elections there were eight candidates representing it. Again a content analysis of the press was useful in indicating reported leaders of both of these movements. For this grouping the additional technique of chain sampling was used.

(*e*) *The three control groups* we used were PACE (Protestant and Catholic Encounter), NUM (New Ulster Movement) and the Campaign for Social Justice in Northern Ireland, which were the intercommunal parties which came to our attention.

This gave an approximate total sample of a hundred people. However, as by this stage it had become clear that there would only be four members of the interviewing team in Ulster for a week, it appeared unlikely that there would be time to interview everybody. Therefore priorities were established within each grouping which were determined by the fact that we were primarily interested in interviewing decision-makers. The priorities in each grouping were:

1. members of the Cabinet;
2. people who had been instrumental in leading the revolt against O'Neill;
3. the successful candidates;

4. those who formed the decision-making cabals within each movement;
5. people in accredited positions within each of the organisations.

Other than this the aim was simply to interview as many people as possible in each group, concentrating first on the first four groupings, and secondly on people residing in Belfast. The latter criterion was inserted in order to save the time that would be spent in tracking down individual members of the sample living in isolated parts of Ulster. In the end Londonderry was also included as an interviewing base as a significant number of the sample were most easily contacted there.

By the end of the week we had interviewed 50 of the sample. Of these 11 were Pro-O'Neill Unionists, 9 were Anti-O'Neill Unionists, 11 were Established Opposition, 13 were Civil Rights/People's Democracy and 6 were members of intercommunal parties.

ULSTER TRIP

The first task was to prepare a historical background to the conflict. A research assistant spent three weeks reading *Keesing's Archives*, available books and the local press and produced a report which provided:

1. A brief history of Ireland, outlining the important dates and events in Ulster's history;
2. an account of the events over the past year leading up to the present situation;
3. an indication of the principal parties to the dispute and their official policies;
4. A short description of how Ulster was administered.

A card was prepared for each member of the sample. This included personal data, political affiliation, result of the February election, extracts from speeches outlining positions on various issues, and, perhaps most important, a photograph and information as to how the subject could be contacted. The photograph proved to be useful when an interviewer at Stormont was expected to be able to recognise an individual among a group of MPs.

The questionnaire had to be piloted to see if the questions were realistic for an Ulster politician. Through the use of personal contacts we were able to arrange an interview with one of the Ulster MPs in Westminster. This proved to be very successful—

the interview lasted for over two hours and extensive answers were given to each of the questions.

An interview team of four was appointed. The project appeared to demand a vast amount of coordination in the field, and any larger unit risked becoming unmanageable. In the light of our experience, this assumption seems to be well founded.

After this a letter was sent to each of the MPs at Stormont. This circulation list was restricted to MPs both because it was impossible to ascertain the exact addresses of other subjects, and also because the Civil Rights/People's Democracy group sample was not finalised until after our arrival. The letter reproduced below, stressed the confidentiality of the interview, which, as discussed later, was one way by which we hoped to make sure that we were obtaining honest replies:

Our unit is concerned with gaining an understanding of how conflicts develop and of how they can be resolved. In order to do this the unit is studying conflicts in international, national and industrial spheres. We are undertaking, as part of this project, a study of the present situation in Ulster.

The main part of the study will consist of interviews with the leaders of the different groups which play an influential role in Ulster life. We hope in fact to send a research team to Belfast at the end of this month to carry out these interviews. We would like to include you among our panel of interviewees. All such interviews will, of course, be treated in the strictest confidence and no document will ever be published which mentions any individual by name. The actual interview will take less than an hour to complete.

Upon our arrival in Belfast a member of our research team will contact you to see if you would be willing to be interviewed.

The next step before leaving was for all the interviewers to practise with the interview schedule in order to standardise the approach and ensure reliability. A set of instructions concerning the use of the interview schedule was also prepared, the most relevant points of which are:

5. During the interview let the subject talk as much as possible. Only when the subject appears to have no more to say on a particular question should you suggest additional issues for him to comment on. If, during the interview, you ask additional questions, please write these down so that one knows which answers belong to which questions.

6. The following are specific guidelines to interviewers on each of the questions:

(a) *Questions 1 and 2*
If the subject doesn't mention them probe: one man one vote; O'Neill's fate; Paisley's position; students' civil rights; demonstration; parliamentary action.

(b) *Questions 3 and 4*
In addition to the points mentioned in 1 and 2, add 'fate of the opposition parties; new parties; new elections; intervention by England.

(c) *Question 5*
If not mentioned, probe: by parliamentary measures; by demonstration; by intervention; civil rights; violence; new political groupings.

(d) *Question 6*
If not mentioned and if relevant, probe: possibility of intervention; make things worse; inhibit change.

(e) *Question 7*
Treat this as a two-part question referring both to Ulster's past history from the seventeenth century to the present, and also to particular events in the past three years which have brought on the present crisis.

(f) *Question 8*
Check IRA and England.

(g) *Question 9*
Simply probe—'can you think of any remark . . . ?'

(h) *Question 10*
Just probe—'can you think of any other ways . . . ?' It may be best to take each of the problems mentioned in Question 9 in turn.

(i) *Question 11*
Simply probe—'can you think of any others . . . ?'

(j) *Question 12*
If there is any hesitation take each of the political parties in turn.

On arrival in Ulster the main task was to contact and make appointments with as many of the sample as possible. Each member of the team was to concentrate on a different grouping. This was partly to prevent two people trying to interview the same politician; a second and perhaps more important reason was that as Ulster is a small and comparatively close-knit community,

especially at the political level, we argued that it would be difficult for people to trust us if they saw the same person interviewing
a Cabinet minister in the morning and a leader of the People's
Democracy in the afternoon. Even though it is possible for the
same person to interview all sides to a dispute, as work in the
industrial field has shown,[7] this cannot be done successfully until
rapport has been built up with all sides, which can take many
months to achieve. We did not have this time, and the best
alternative appeared to be to have each interviewer concentrating
on one faction. This procedure also proved beneficial in gaining
access, as when the confidence of one or two key people had
been gained they would help to arrange subsequent interviews.

We had three main ways of establishing initial contacts. The
first was through the pilot interview at which we had been given
an introduction to one of the pro-O'Neill groups. This person
besides granting an interview arranged that on the following
afternoon one of the team should meeet him at Stormont where
he would provide introductions to any MPs who were about.
This meeting turned out to be a rather traumatic experience of
standing in a corridor where the member would grab hold of a
passing MP and say, 'Could I introduce you to . . . .', and then
rush off. This left the interviewer to establish rapport with a
member who was obviously hurrying from one place to another
and who, despite the letters that had been sent to all MPs beforehand, had never heard of the survey. However, in most cases it
was possible to arrange subsequent times for the subjects to be
interviewed.

The second approach was through Queen's University. We
had heard before we left that there were academics there who
were concerned with the political situation and we had written
beforehand and arranged to meet them on the day of our arrival.
They proved to be very friendly and willing to help, and were
instrumental in setting up the initial links with the People's
Democracy grouping, and also with the NILP.

The third approach, and the one we used most, was the telephone, either to a private number or to the House of Parliament.
It normally took about six calls to track down any single individual since first there were often many individuals of the same
name in the book and secondly there was always a "front"
person to get past, i.e. wife or secretary. When we eventually
spoke to the subject we introduced ourselves along the lines of
the original letter sent to the MPs and asked if we could make
an appointment. Again, in nearly all cases this proved possible.

It was difficult to coordinate all of the interviews. This resulted from the fact that the interviewing sites were concentrated around Belfast, i.e. Stormont, the hotel, offices and private homes. We had one hire car between four of us and this often meant that one was having to act part of the time as a chauffeur shuffling interviewers from one appointment to another, all being co-ordinated through one team member sitting in the hotel bedroom.

The interview itself was often done under less than favourable conditions. This point will be taken up in more detail later in the chapter, when we consider the general problems of fieldwork thrown up by the study. At this stage it is sufficient to indicate that we had to interview people where and when the interviewer could get hold of them. This was particularly so in the case of the People's Democracy/Civil Rights grouping, as they had no proper offices.

While the average time spent on each interview was an hour, we had to allow more than this when making arrangements. Allowance had to be made for travel time which involved not only getting to and from the interview but often difficulty in finding addresses, and then finding a place to park one's car. Though these might appear to be trivial details, they are over-looked at the risk of missing an interview. Also, in many cases time, perhaps quarter of an hour or so, had to be spent in establish-ing rapport, saying who we were and what we wanted the in-formation for. Though we were officially from the London School of Economics, we introduced ourselves as being attached to the University of London. This was for the practical reason that the ruling establishment in Ulster identified the trouble-makers as being motivated by an international conspiracy of Trotskyist radicals whose headquarters were the LSE. A third time factor was that an hour had to be left at the end of each interview in case it ran over time.

THE DUBLIN TRIP

As our knowledge of the conflict in Ulster increased, it became more apparent that in order to understand it properly we had to take into consideration parties outside Ulster. One reason for this is the tendency of intercommunal conflicts to drag in other parties. The two most relevant in this case were Eire and Britain. Whereas it was possible to gain some idea of the attitudes of the British Government towards Ulster from an analysis of the British press and from informal conversations with civil servants, we realised that we had very little idea of how the leading groups in Eire perceived the situation in the North and why they had adopted their actual positions. We therefore decided that a study comparable to that carried out in the North would help to fill this gap.

In planning it we were again restricted, for financial and administrative reasons, to one person in the field for a single week. This severely limited the sample and we decided that instead of doing one or two groups in depth, we would try to obtain interviews with leaders of as many different groups as possible.

As before we employed a research assistant for two weeks to draw up a background to the situation in Eire. This included historical links, reported statements by political and other leaders, and any action by the Government or others over Ulster. Political parties were identified by the June 1969 elections which showed that in the Dail (the Dublin Houses of Parliament), were that the ruling party, the Fianna Fáil, had seventy-five seats, the Fine Gael fifty, Labour eighteen, and Independent one. In addition to Members of Parliament, the other groupings that appeared important were extra-parliamentary parties such as the Sinn Fein and the IRA, the trade unions, the religious leaders and the press. It was decided to include the press on this occasion because there was a significantly lower state of tension in Dublin than in Belfast. There was much less risk of there being any public statement about our work and even if a statement had been issued, it would not have created as much controversy. A third reason for working with the press was that through the Irish Embassy in London it was possible to obtain personal introductions to key people and this again reduced the risk of inadvertent reporting.

As we wanted to compare the data obtained in this study with that from the earlier one in Belfast, we tried to keep the questions as similar as possible.

1. How would you describe the present troubles in the Six Counties?
2. Could you briefly indicate what you think are the critical points in Irish history which have led to the present situation?
3. As regards the political situation what would you like to see happen in the Six Counties in the next three months?
4. Now speaking realistically what do you actually expect will happen in the Six Counties in the next three months?
5. Now considering the next five years, what developments, if any, would you like to see happen?

6. Again, speaking realistically, what do you think will happen in the Six Counties over the next five years?
7. Given what you would like to see happen in the Six Counties in the future, what do you think are the most effective ways to achieve these aims?
8. What can the Irish (Eire) Government and people do about what is happening in the Six Counties and what courses of action either have been or are likely to be adopted?
9. What do you think of the English intervention into the Six Counties and what in your opinion is the English Government likely to do next?
10. What effects is the present trouble in the Six Counties likely to have in Eire?
11. What other forces or countries besides Eire and England are likely to intervene in the Six Counties and why?
12. How would you describe each of the different groups of people that play an important part in the Six Counties' present problems?

As in Ulster, the majority of our interviews were arranged through a barrage of telephone calls. In addition, the Irish Embassy in London had previously arranged interviews with members of the Department of External Affairs and the press. Owing to the limited time, the priorities were to obtain interviews with the leader, deputy leader and foreign affairs spokesman of each of the political parties. By the end of the week fifteen interviews were carried out. Four of these were with the Fianna Fáil (one with an ex-Minister), two with Labour MPs and two with Fine Gael MPs. One interview was carried out with the editor of a leading paper, one with a representative of the Sinn Fein, one with a trade union spokesman, three with members of the Department of External Affairs and one with a member of the British Foreign Office.

INTERVIEWING PROBLEMS

This section discusses problems which arose while we were carrying out the interviews.

(a) Processing information

Open-ended questions like ours encourage respondents to talk very freely. It then becomes impossible to take a longhand verbatim record. Ideally we should have used one of two alternatives; either interviewers competent in shorthand or tape recorders. The first are difficult to find while tape recorders in many cases have an inhibiting effect. Given that neither alternative was used all the answers are an edited version distorted in terms of what the interviewer thought most important.

(b) Confidentiality

The specific problem relates to the fact that quite often when the interview was ostensibly finished, the respondent would say: 'Now, here's something else but please don't write this down.' What does the interviewer do? Does he consider this to be additional information of the same kind as that given in the answers to the questionnaire—that is, does the agreement that we are interested in finding out as much as possible about the conflict and that we will use this information without mentioning names, still hold? On the other hand, is this information of a completely different order in that it is not to be used at all? But if it is not to be used at all, why were we told it in the first place, given that we had not asked for it? When interviewees say "please don't write this down," do they mean that under no conditions should it be traceable back, whereas when they answer the other questions they may be structuring their replies to protect themselves in case their words could ever be traceable back to source. In most cases this additional information concerned specific details of the conflict, for example a description of what happened in a particular civil rights march, and as such was not really relevant to our questions as it only served to build up an overall picture of what the conflict was about. The point about the phrase, 'please don't write this down', is that it is not the same as saying, 'please don't tell this to anybody else'; the latter implies that this is something between speaker and interviewer, while the former says, 'this is a point of view which I don't want known to be ascribed to me. In such cases the remarks were recorded after the interview had ended.

(c) Coordination between interviewers

The success of the field study depended on the interviewing group being small and flexible. It was essential to be able to keep track of who had interviewed whom, of which people had been contacted, of when and where appointments had been fixed, so that:

1. there was no clash of interviews;
2. all interviews in one area were carried out at the same time; for example that all the interviews in Londonderry were arranged on the same day so that they could be accomplished in one trip;
3. maximum use could be made of the contacts we had built up. If one interviewer had found that a subject was a particularly busy man and could only be contacted at a particular place, or if someone else was known to be a difficult person and the best way to approach him was by going through a third person, it was obviously essential to be able to transfer this information;
4. there was also a need for coordination between the interviews in the field and the person making appointments in the hotel.

All of this required that the team was small enough to keep in constant touch with each other.

(d) Interviewing sites

As mentioned earlier, the interviews were carried out under a wide variety of conditions—hotel bedrooms, pub lounges, the MPs' tea room, and so on, each of which created its own problems, mainly in manœuvring the subject so that he was in a position where his answers could not be overheard and where other people walking past could not catch his eye and distract him. In one case this involved making sure that the subject had his back to a television crew waiting to interview him and, as the interviewer could see looking over his shoulder, urgently signalling to him to come as the light rapidly faded. One specific point of interest which struck the interviewers was the remoteness and grandeur of Stormont in comparison with the rest of Belfast and Ulster, and consequently how easy it must be for someone who spent any length of time there to grow out of touch with what was happening in the rest of the country.

(e) Validity

The question here is whether subjects said what they really believed. They probably combine the image that they wish to present of themselves to the interviewer and the image which they want him to have of the conflict. To the extent that the interviewer is a neutral figure, there is the possibility that these are the images the interviewees themselves operate with most of the time. Nobody will necessarily have a constant image of either themselves or the conflict, given all its aspects; all one can hope for is to obtain the most consistent image, i.e. that on which the person operates most of the time. We believe that in most cases we obtained this, primarily because of the precautions we took. As already indicated these included dividing up the interviewing team, and of telling the subjects that we were not reporters and that any information they gave us could not be used to change the outcome of the situation. Other reasons for our belief are that we were in many cases told evidence which, if we had reported it, would have been incriminating to the person concerned. We were also frequently asked by subjects for reassurance that we were not journalists and that what they said would not be attributed. In addition we took precautions to make sure that any information that we obtained could not be 'stolen', i.e. all the questionnaires were sent back to England at the end of each day. Even though it might seem slightly paranoid, we had some evidence by the end of our stay that members of the team who were interviewing the People's Democracy/Civil Rights group were having their movements checked.

CO-OPERATION OF SUBJECTS

Taking both the Dublin and the Ulster trips together, we had fewer than half a dozen refusals, excluding people who were out of the country at the time. Of those who gave a reason, two said they were too busy, and one that it would not be appropriate, given his position. The question then arises: 'Why, when we had been told that we would find it difficult to gain access, were so many people who theoretically should have been very busy, prepared to give us on the average an hour of their time?' It is possible to reverse the question and say: 'Why should they not?' People in countries which have not yet suffered from the plague of social science questionnaires still find it flattering that people should want to ask them for their views on a situation and, provided these are going to be treated in confidence, why should not they say what they believe?

Another reason suggested to us is that in a crisis there is normally no one to whom a participant can talk and try out ideas and opinions. This is because if one of the definitions of a conflict situation is that all people are committed, even if only to the extent that they are committed to being uncommitted, then it is dangerous to speak with other than a public face. A confidential interview also enables a person to adopt a pose closer to his true beliefs.

THE FINANCIAL AND TIME COST OF THE INTERVIEWS[8]

We calculated in terms of time and money how much each of the sixty-five interviews had cost. This costing covered a pre-interview stage which included the gathering of background information and the design and piloting of the questionnaires; the interview stage, involving the field trips and all attendant expenses; and a post-interview stage which covered the transcribing of the interviews up to the stage where they were ready for data analysis. The average interview worked out at approximately thirteen hours and cost £10·70.

LONDONDERRY RIOTS

In August of 1969 *New Society* invited John Bayley and Peter Loizos[9] to go to Belfast and Londonderry to report on the riots. They spent three days there, a large part of it inside Bogside, and were able to observe the arrival of the 'B'-Specials followed shortly afterwards by the British troops. They were also in Belfast at the time the subsequent rioting broke out. Their study[10] yielded useful insights at a micro level into the development of conflict situations.

[1] See for example, P. Gordon Walker, *The Cabinet*, Cape, 1970.

[2] F. C. Bartlett, *Remembering*, Cambridge University Press, 1932.

[3] L. Festinger, *A Theory of Cognitive Dissonance*, Harper & Row, 1957.

[4] E. Goffman, *The Presentation of Self in Everyday Life*, Doubleday, 1959.

[5] R. K. Merton and Patricia Kendall, 'The focused interview', *American Journal of Sociology*, li, 541–2.

[6] R. Jenkins, 'Perception in crisis', Paper read at International Peace Research Association conference, Sweden, 1967.

[7] A. N. Oppenheim and J. C. R. Bayley, 'Productivity and conflict', *Proceedings of Third I.P.R.A. conference.*

[8] R. S. P. Wiener, 'The financial and time cost of interviewing political élites', *Bulletin of British Psychology*, lxxiii 29. (1970)

[9] Lecturer in Social Anthropology, London School of Economics.

[10] J. Bayley and P. Loizos, 'Bogside off its knees', *New Society*, 21 August 1969.

5

The identification of parties and issues to a conflict

The previous chapter described the way parties to the conflict were identified when the project started. By the time the data analysis began, this approach was found to be too simple. We subsequently developed a different way to analyse conflicts and identify the relevant parties. This new framework became the basis for the interpretation of the interview data given in Chapter 6.

INTRODUCTION

The conflict in Ulster, like any conflict, is composed of many different elements—Protestant working class v Catholic working class; Right Wing Unionists v moderate Unionists; Dublin v Stormont; Westminster v Stormont; economic development v civil unrest; those who want change through parliamentary procedures v those who want change through extra-parliamentary methods.

The new framework enables this complexity to be broken down into its basic constituent parts. In essence, the framework lays down that:

(a) conflict is composed of a number of disputes which are themselves made up of a number of issues. This is best illustrated by using factor analysis as an analogy where the issues become the basic variables, the disputes the factors and the conflict the sum of all these factors.

(b) The normal approach to political parties, treating them as comparatively unified organisations, fails to show that conflict embraces a number of individuals and organisations who are in agreement on some issues and in opposition on others. To get at this level parties have to be redefined in terms of the specific individuals or groups which participants to the conflict perceive to play a part in each issue.

(c) The issues at stake in a conflict and the parties involved change over time and therefore any analysis of a conflict has to be carried out at set intervals over its duration.

The rest of this chapter examines each of these points in more detail and looks at the methodological difficulties they pose.

DERIVATION OF THE ISSUES

How can the issues to a conflict be ascertained? Anything that participants in the conflict mention or refer to in connection with the situation is a relevant issue. This information can be obtained in various ways. The one preferred in this study is where the participants, through interviews or questionnaires, themselves define the intent of the conflict. Any alternative method involves the analyst assuming that either on theoretical or practical grounds he is in a better position to undersand the conflict than are the participants. As we discuss below, there is a place for the analyst's knowledge, but this is in addition to rather than instead of that of the participants. Another way of arriving at the basic issues is by content analysis of the mass media and a study of the relevant documents, books, parliamentary papers, articles and so on.

COPING WITH LARGE NUMBERS OF ISSUES

The next step is to reduce the almost infinite number of possible issues to a manageable quantity. The total number of issues will be a function of the method by which they were reached. In this study, because we restricted our sample to political leaders and asked each of them only twelve questions, a manageable number of issues was produced. If the sample had been larger and the questions more comprehensive, steps would have had to be taken to reduce the increased number of issues. This can be done by restricting the study to a single aspect of the conflict and considering only the issues relevant to it. A second way is to produce an index of centrality, which will largely be composed of the frequency with which each issue is mentioned, on the assumption that the more frequently an issue is given the more central it must be to the conflict. 'Central' is here defined in terms of people's perceptions. It might well be the case that an issue which few people mention will prove to be the key in providing an end to the dispute. At this initial stage of analysis, however, the only criteria that can be adopted are those of the participants.

IDENTIFICATION OF DISPUTES

Once all the issues have been agreed on, the next step is to link them together into the disputes. This can be done in a variety of ways.

(a) The first is factor analysis—each issue can be correlated with every other issue and then analysed to see if any factors or basic groupings of issues emerge. A difficulty with this approach arises when the sample interviewed is very small; there are then far more variables or issues than subjects, and this makes a factor analytic approach difficult, if not impossible. Also in such a case there will be a large number of issues which each have only a few respondents, and this too will create computational problems. A way round this is to take the intermediate step of devising a set of coding categories for the issues. The categories can be treated either as a type of first order factor or simply as a set of preliminary groups of data. One then correlates each category with the others and derives basic factors or disputes from them.

(b) A second way is to link the variables on some theoretical basis. One can for example take a Marxist position or a systems theory approach and group the issues in terms of the particular theory.

At the end of this stage, the analyst ought to be in a position to identify the main disputes which make up the conflict and which issues are relevant to which disputes. Many of the issues, particularly in the factorial approach, will lead on to more than one dispute, but this should be a differential loading in so far as they will correlate more highly with one factor than another. The identification or labelling of a dispute can then be done in terms of the issues which have the highest loading. The two procedures outlined above can also be used to link the disputes together into a meaningful pattern.

CONFLICT AS AN ONGOING STATE OF AFFAIRS

We have so far only been looking at the conflict in terms of a single cross-sectional analysis. However, conflicts are continually changing phenomena and an issue at one stage might subsequently phase out. To be able to perceive this dynamic aspect it is necessary to study the conflict at repeated intervals. By adopting similar samples, procedures and questions at each stage, a picture can be built up of how the conflict changes. It becomes clear that after analysing only two stages in a conflict we have three sets of issues to explain—two sets composed of what was said at each stage and a third set composed of the differences between what was relevant at one stage and what was relevant at the next. These differences can also be treated as a set of issues. It is unlkely that it will be meaningful to factor analyse these issues and it is here that the analyst's knowledge of the dynamic processes of conflict should be particularly relevant in grouping the issues into a meaningful pattern. This same knowledge will be equally useful in a retrospective analysis showing the causes which led to the particular pattern of issues and disputes emerging at each stage. Ideally, the present study should have included at least one follow up to enable such a dynamic analysis to be incorporated into the results. Lack of time, money and personnel prevented this.

THE DEFINITION OF PARTIES

Once the conflict has been analysed into its constituent disputes and issues it becomes possible to analyse the parties which make up the conflict. The term 'political party' is normally applied to a formal, representative structure or 'set of decision-making roles acknowledged by the majority of party members as representing their views',[1] encompassing organisations and/or individuals with basically similar values. Examples of this definition would be the Unionist Party, the Northern Ireland Labour Party and so on. No one would deny that these are parties to the Ulster conflict —but as we have seen it is composed of many different disputes and issues. Does it make sense to say that both these are parties to all the disputes and issues? For argument's sake let us assume that one of the disputes is *discrimination against Catholics*; issues which have high loadings on this include gerrymandering, job discrimination, and 'B' Specials as a Protestant private army.

The Unionist party is obviously concerned with all these issues, and its headquarters produces literature outlining the party's position on each. Similarly each of the other political parties has at various times taken a public stand on these issues. The normal methodological procedure would be to take each of these statements and show where the parties differed and from this account for the dissension between the Northern Ireland political parties.

Such an approach presents a vastly oversimplified picture of the situation—for a number of reasons:

1. There is no such thing as a unified party. Not only will different individuals and groups within a party differ in their views from issue to issue, but they will also differ on the same issue. There was a split in the Unionist Party over the need to retain the 'B' Specials and a much more important one over whether O'Neill should stay or go. Therefore treating parties as single entities emphasises differences between them and glosses over internal differences.

2. Individuals can be members of more than one party at the same time. Some of the opposition are members of Stormont while being executive members of the Civil Rights Association. An individual could therefore take one stand on gerrymandering in his role as a parliamentarian and another in his role as a Civil Rights campaigner. The above definition of parties ignores this whole area of overlapping roles.

3. An official party will always try to present a unified political outlook and is therefore likely to take a position in regard to a dispute rather than to its constituent issues. This overlooks the fact that many individual members will follow the party line on one issue in a dispute but disagree with it on others.

4. Official parties are comparatively static entities while a conflict is always in a state of constant flux. New issues are always rising, more information is given about old issues, incidents occur and so on. This means that individual members within a party are often changing their positions on different issues even though the official party line stays unaltered.

5. The final point is that very often individuals in seemingly opposed parties will agree on many issues. The approach emphasises differences rather than similarities between parties.

In order to penetrate this complexity to show the dynamic patterns of interaction that exist at the issue level, it is necessary to redefine what is meant by a party. *A party can be defined in systems terms as the smallest unit, whether individual or grouping of individuals, which is identified by either an analyst or the participants as being connected with that issue.*

The easiest way of identifying such parties is to ask the participants themselves to list all groups and/or individuals relevant to the issue under discussion. This approach has the shortcoming that there might well be groups who believe that a particular issue has relevance to them, even though none of the subjects questioned believe this to be the case. The smaller the sample interviewed the more likely this is to happen.

The other approach is for the observer to begin identifying parties to each of the issues by, for example, a content analysis of the mass media and other documents. This produces two major problems:

The first of these is the criterion to be adopted. Are parties to an issue defined in terms of (a) those who can influence it; (b) those who are affected by it; or (c) those whose position needs to be known in order to understand it?

Let us take the issue of 'B' Specials. Who can influence it? There are the Orange Order, the Unionist Party, the RUC, Arthur Young, Chichester-Clark, the Cabinet, the IRA, Westminster, Fianna Fáil and so on. However, the stand any of these take might well be determined by their supporters. Many Unionist MPs, for example, are forced to take a hard line because of grass-root opinion. Does the latter then constitute a party to the issue?

If we now extend the survey to include all who might be affected by this issue then we could include virtually the whole population of Ulster. Though looking at the problem in this way can help to define the boundaries of any issue, it can do little to differentiate which are the relevant parties. The alternative is to decide on a cutoff point, i.e. Catholics who actually demonstrated were much more likely to be affected by the 'B' Specials than those who stayed indoors.

If we include all of those whose position we need to know to understand the issue fully we must obtain, for example, a breakdown of the 'B' Specials themselves, in terms of their motives, aims and composition.

The second major problem is how to determine the size of the smallest unit. Let us revert to the example of the 'B' Specials. The RUC and the Ulster Cabinet are two groups concerned with this issue. At the extreme level each member of the RUC and each Cabinet minister would affect and be affected by the 'B' Specials. Yet it is clear that not only would it be impossible to interview all members of the RUC but that the individual members would in most conditions have much less effect on the issue than members of the Unionist Cabinet. Does the observer, therefore, take individual members, subgroups or the whole group as the smallest unit?

Both patterns can be largely solved by introducing a weighting system. Let us presume that we are interested in parties who can produce a change in the 'B' Specials. Again, we can list some of them: the Ulster Cabinet, Unionist MPs, the Civil Rights Association, RUC and so on.

Let us start with the Cabinet. At the time of the study it could be divided into Pro-O'Neill Unionists, Anti-O'Neill Unionists and O'Neill himself. In the observer's perception of the parties' capability to influence events concerning the 'B' Specials it would make sense to treat each of these three elements as one basic unit. Among the Unionist MPs there were some individuals, such as Craig, with a lot of support who would therefore again need to be treated as basic units. Many of the other MPs could be treated collectively as a single unit. Similarly, in the Civil Rights Association, there would be some individuals, such as Hume, who would be a single unit, while the remainder of the Civil Rights Association would be taken as another unit. Finally, the whole of the RUC could be taken as another basic unit.

Such a measure as this must be subjective and approximate. It does however mean that it is possible to take an issue and ask who will affect it, and, by weighting the parties, to include all the possible groupings balanced in a crude manner in the degree to which they are perceived to be able to influence it. Some of the shortcomings of this approach can be overcome by taking into consideration the time dimension, analysing what has happened over a nine-month period and thus seeing how much influence each of the parties has had and adjusting the weighting accordingly.

As we have suggested, most of the problems arise when the observer alone decides who are the parties to an issue. A much safer strategy is for the participants to define the parties and for the observer to add to them only when his specialised training indicates that the participants have possibly overlooked groups. Such a situation might occur when an observer with experience from another intercommunal situation realised that if events were to follow the same pattern a group of previously uninvolved people would find themselves part of the conflict.

An additional difficulty is how to refer to groups of individuals so that they are in some way discernible on that issue from all other parties. The easiest way to do this is by using the official tags, such as RUC for groups which are treated as a single basic unit. However, it becomes virtually impossible to talk of the Unionist organisation as a party to a dispute, as in nearly all cases the observers would be interested in the attitudes of its component subgroups. This difficulty is accentuated when we realise that so far we have only been considering the parties which interact with one issue of one dispute in a conflict. As we have seen, a conflict is composed of many disputes which are themselves divisible into a number of more basic issues. Issues relevant to one party will be ignored by another. Similarly the basic unit of a party will vary from issue to issue. In talking about the 'B' Specials it makes sense to differentiate between the Paisleyites and Anti-O'Neill Unionists but if the issue was partition then all non-moderate Protestants might be classed together as a basic unit. Therefore classification of any party must be flexible enough to cover the changes in the composition of parties to different issues.

ATTITUDE OF A PARTY TO AN ISSUE

After establishing that a party is relevant to a particular issue, the next step is to determine that party's attitude or behaviour towards the issue. It is important to differentiate public and private stands, for it is possible, for example, for Unionists privately to wish the border to be abolished, but for political reasons to act as if it were a permanent institution. Consequently, some circumstances may force parties to appear to be in conflict when in private they might agree on many things. It is these unspoken beliefs which the analyst should aim to discover. The most direct way, as done in this study, is to carry out confidential interviews with all the identified parties.

Methodological problems arise in dealing with parties where the basic unit is larger than the individual. Suppose it were decided that the Pro-O'Neill Unionists were a party to the 'B' Special issue, and suppose further that interviews showed a wide degree of disagreement between the individual group members. If we had already decided to treat them collectively as a basic unit and therefore concluded that individually they were unlikely to affect the issue significantly, then the only solution would be to produce a mean or average position.

An additional problem arises in dealing with a much larger basic unit, such as the RUC. It is obviously impossible in practice to interview all the 8,200 RUC members. The simplest solution is to accept the opinion of the organisation's spokesman as being representative of all people in his group, unless one has evidence to the contrary. Even though this will mean that differences within that party will be glossed over, it is practically impossible, though theoretically desirable, to include every single difference. In this case the analyst will have to decide which differences are important for each issue, and therefore the size of the appropriate unit.

GROUPING OF PARTIES

Having determined the attitudes that each party holds towards an issue the next step is to group the parties in some way. The simplest way is to pool together all the parties that have common attitudes to an issue. This will show, first, the complexity of conflict situations; not only will the composition of groups of parties be changing from issue to issue but also parties which are agreed on one issue will be opposed on others. Secondly, it will serve to indicate how officially labelled parties which appear in terms of the total conflict to be in disagreement can, when broken down into smaller units, have much common ground.

A second step is to factor analyse the parties. The analysis will show whether there are any underlying groupings of parties which will account for the pattern of answers. This step is of course similar to groupings of issues into disputes.

So far we have only been considering parties to an issue. It is, of course, possible to determine parties to a dispute. Once issues have been grouped into disputes, then it is possible to take the parties to the issues which load highest on the dispute and thus determine those most relevant to that dispute.

Another point which was discussed earlier in connection with disputes, but which needs further ramification here, is the time dimension. So far in our discussion of parties the analysis has been in cross-sectional terms. As we saw earlier, the issues to a conflict can be expected to change over time. When this happens it will naturally produce changes in the parties to the conflict— new basic units will emerge, groupings of parties about issues will alter. It is in order to grasp this complexity that the ideal study should be repeated every nine months or so.

PROBLEMS OF RELIABILITY AND VALIDITY

When all the parties to an issue have been interviewed, the usual problems of coding, reliability and validity arise. As we mentioned earlier, the coding scheme can be taken as a preliminary step for grouping all the issues. The relevance of theory comes in explaining the emerging pattern of issues and disputes.

Reliability is especially important in the analysis of open-ended questions. In our case, after the sets of categories had been devised, all the questions were coded twice by different individuals. There was basic disagreement between them on only

I

9·5 per cent of the items. There was also an error reliability of 13·5 per cent which included items either being missed or being accidentally placed in the wrong category.

Even though items can be reliably coded, validity can still be a problem. Take for example the statement, 'The Catholics aren't too bad'. Does this mean, 'I really dislike Catholics and this is a polite way of saying so', or that 'On the whole I like Catholics'? It is possible for there to be high reliability in the coding of this item—both judges might agree that the speaker really liked Catholics—but a second interview might show that in fact he hated them. With problems like this validity checks can be built into the analysis by comparing the answers with other statements made by the subject or by seeing if certain background variables show up, e.g. membership of the Orange Order and so on.

THE PRESENT STUDY IN RELATION TO THE IDENTIFICATION OF PARTIES

As the interview study was carried out before the development of the theoretical approach just outlined, it deviates from it on a number of points. Appendix 1 records the political leaders' perception of the basic issues in the Ulster conflict. These issues are the categories that made best sense of the answers to the twelve appended questions. Even though the range of issues is vast, it must be realised that this picture of the conflict is limited by the fact that the sample was restricted to leaders and that there were only twelve questions. If a wider sample had been included different issues might have emerged and issues already mentioned might have varied in importance. Similarly the span of questions must focus the range of answers, but in so far as the questions were open-ended and covered past, present and future aspects of the conflict this bias probably had less influence on the total picture.

The normal procedure for finding the underlying disputes which make up the conflict would have been to factor analyse these issues. It was not possible to do this because, in a study of political leaders, there were too few subjects and too many variables. We were in this case forced to adopt alternative solutions:

(a) The first was to use a simple frequency measure—the disputes were those issues which were mentioned most often. Even though this approach cannot discover underlying patterns among the variables it does indicate the issues which sprang most readily to people's minds. The result of this analysis is given in Appendix 2 and included with it are scores of how frequently the official parties mentioned each of these disputes.

(b) The second approach was to correlate every issue with every other issue in each question and then apply the chi square test of significance. Ideally each issue should have been correlated with issues in all other questions but even the more limited approach yielded well over a million lines of computer output, with, as Appendix 3 shows, very few significant results. This again was due to the smallness of the sample and the large number of issues, as it meant that for most issues there were only four or five respondents. This approach, while not providing anything like as complete a picture of relations between issues as would a factor analytic programme, does enable the observer to see what, if any, correlations exist between pairs of issues. The more frequently any one issue is significantly correlated with others, the more central it can be assumed to be and the more likely it is to be a dispute to the conflict.

These two approaches are obviously related because only if an issue is mentioned frequently is there likely to be a sufficient spread of answers to make any statistical test significant. One advantage of the second approach is that it enables the observer to identify the individuals who perceive relationships to hold between any pairs of issues. When trying to initiate new ideas in a situation it is just as useful to know how a person perceives issues to go together as it is to know his opinion an any one issue.

The next stage of our analysis, the identification of each of the issues, was greatly simplified. The greatest problem, that of determining the basic unit of a party and its appropriate weighting, was cancelled out, through our sample being of political leaders. This meant that the basic unit was the individual and that all, being leaders, had equal weighting. This of course is to some extent an artificial measure as the answers to Q. 12 (Appendix 1) showed. Subjects, when asked who were the groups and individuals who made up the conflict, gave fifty-seven different groups and individuals. In any more comprehensive follow-up study these would have to be taken as the starting point for identifying the parties to the conflict.

The second step in the procedure, that of working out which parties were affected by what issue, was solved by the simple expedient of letting the respondents define this themselves. Thus if a subject mentioned an issue he was *ipso facto* a party to that issue. This approach, because of the restricted sample, means that many parties to each of the issues were not included. It also meant that the criterion we used was not who affects or is affected by an issue but a perceptual one—any party which mentions an issue must feel that this is an important issue both to itself and to the conflict. In the ideal state of affairs the next step would have been simply to tabulate the parties to each of the issues. It would then have been possible to show how the groupings of parties varied from issue to issue and how people from opposing 'official' parties were in many cases allied. This would have allowed a very precise analysis of the conflict; one could have gone through it, issue by issue, and seen which groups of parties were in favour and which were opposed—extremely useful knowledge for anybody wishing either to instigate or to delay change, whether social or political. It was not possible to do this because of the pledge of confidentiality given to the subjects. Any attempt to make a meaningful comparison of individual parties was therefore impossible within this limitation.

The fallback position was to revert to grouping individuals by their official party labels and see how they divided on each of the central issues or disputes. The results are given in Appendix 2. It was only possible to do this for the disputes and not for each of the issues because of the low number of responses to most of the individual issues. Even though, as previously mentioned, this technique places undue emphasis on differences between parties, it still shows some of the similarities that exist. The final step in the identification of parties was to factor analyse them, taking the responses of all the parties to all the issues and seeing if there were any underlying groupings of parties which would explain the pattern of answers. The intention was to see whether the parties' responses indicated that there was a more functional grouping than that of official parties.

This chapter has attempted to show that in a dynamic conflict situation the analyst requires a more flexible unit of analysis than the static official party structure which hides more than it reveals. Such a unit of analysis involves a breakdown of the conflict into its basic parts and a building up of the individuals and groups concerned with each part or issue into new groupings of parties. Finally the chapter has shown how the present study comes some way to following these procedures and indicates the areas where it falls short and the reasons.

[1] C. R. Mitchell, *The Identification of Parties to a Dispute*, CAC, 1969 (mimeographed).

6

The results and Northern Ireland

This chapter follows the framework outlined in Chapter 5. The basic issues to the conflict are given and are grouped into the disputes which make up the conflict. The official party attitudes to each of the disputes follow, then a brief account of how the individuals group around the issues. Finally, factor analysis is used to discuss new ways of grouping individual leaders. At each stage there is a discussion of how the findings aid an understanding of the conflict.

THE ISSUES

The first stage of the analysis involved the design of categories to code the answers given to the twelve open-ended questions. The categories, or basic issues to the conflict, are given in Appendix 1. These issues are the points that the political leaders felt were important in understanding the conflict. As the results show there were approximately forty issues to each of the questions. The appendix also shows how many of the leaders mentioned each of the issues. Before going on to consider the issues as answers to each of the questions asked, there are certain points to make about their sheer quantity.

It is very difficult for anybody to gain a full picture unless he has access to all groups within the conflict. This is because many of the issues are mentioned by only two or three subjects and therefore the more restricted the number of contacts with parties the more likely one is to have a distorted picture of the conflict.

In Ulster the British Home Office has always had difficulty in keeping in touch. Before the advent of British troops the main contact was Stormont which was hardly likely to say that it was losing touch with the situation. Evidence that this communication line resulted in a distorted perception of the actual state of affairs, is found in the difficulty that the Eire Foreign Minister

had in persuading the Foreign Office that the Apprentice Boys
March in August 1969 would result in widespread bloodshed.[1]
Westminster's contacts are unlikely to have increased much with
the arrival of British troops. They are, for reasons which will be
discussed later, largely distrusted by the Catholics, whom they
tend to see as the troublemakers. Even though the Home Office
now has its own people in Stormont, much of the political action
originates outside the parliamentary sphere.

ISSUES BY QUESTIONS

The first two questions asked about the short-term desires and
expectations of the political leaders, and the next two about the
longer, five-year perspective.

(a) Difference between expectations and wants

The answers present a gloomy picture of people having a clear
idea of what they want to see happen but very low expectations
that it will be realised in either the short or the long term. In
the short term for example thirteen wanted extensive reform but
only one expected it, while in the long term, twice as many
wanted extensive local government, socio-economic and educational reforms as expected it. This difference between wants and
expectations can only lead to a sense of frustration, to a degree
of disillusionment with the present structures for instituting
change. That this was occurring is illustrated by the fact that
while in the short term seventeen people wanted change to occur
through the parliamentary process, only one person expected
that it would.

There was a sense of fatalism about the findings. For example
only three wanted trouble in the short term, but thirty-five
expected it would occur; in the long term, thirteen expected it
and only one wanted it. Similarly while seven wanted less stern
measures in the long run, only one expected this. It must be
remembered that the sample we interviewed was drawn from
the political leaders and this difference between wants and expectations shows quite clearly the way events had moved beyond
the control of people at the centre. This throws doubt on any
hope of trying to induce change solely through Stormont. If the
situation is such that what matters is determined by various local
leaders, then this is the level where the problem must be tackled.
It is interesting to note that in the long term while only four

wanted disunity within the Unionist party, eleven expected it, while eleven both wanted and expected a growth in Opposition unity. This is one case where expectations appear at the time of writing (September 1970) to have been fulfilled—the Unionist party is still split between its various wings, while members of the Opposition parties have come together in the Social and Democratic Labour Party. This alteration of the political groups is important, provided the split in the Unionist party is decisive enough to produce two separate parties and the Opposition can remain unified. This is because there is now a chance of a radical restructuring of the political divisions, away from religion, towards a class framework.

(b) Differences between short-term and long-term expectations and wants

The situation appears different from this set of answers, for while cooperation with Eire is not even an issue in the short term, in the long term ten want it to happen and nine expect it. Whereas only three want this to go as far as the elimination of the border in the short term, eleven want it in the long term, and of these five expect it to occur. Moves towards economic integration in Europe will play a part in making the border an anachronism. Linked to this is the finding that while only one person expects increased Catholic participation in Ulster's affairs in the short term, seven expect it to occur in the longer perspective.

There is also a long term expectation that as the Unionist party continues to disintegrate the Opposition will continue to unify. Tied in with this, the fear of either a Protestant or Catholic backlash which was an issue in the short term is no longer so in the long term, and similarly only a quarter as many expect there to be stern Government measures on law and order in the long run, compared with the present situation. This change is probably due to the expectation that in the long term there would be either direct or indirect intervention from Westminster.

These figures suggest that at least in certain areas, such as cooperation with the South, things will improve as time passes. Further support for this finding comes from the fact that while in the short term thirty-five people expected trouble, only thirteen did so in the long term, and an improvement in community relations which was not even a possiblity in the short term became so in the longer term.

The answers therefore appear to indicate that looking as far ahead as five years, the present situation will improve, though may be not as much as people hope. There is a danger in accepting optimism at face value. Given present conditions, the future tends to be seen as improving, but the problem is that often the future never comes and people remain caught in the present. The participants can see the final goal but can never overcome the immediate problems of distrust, adequate social change and so on which have to be solved if the goal is to be reached.

MEANS TO ACHIEVE EXPECTATIONS

Subjects were next asked (Q. 5) how they would achieve their expectations. Twelve different remedies were suggested, among them intervention from outside, change of leadership, increasing secularisation and Unionist reform. There was little unanimity on any one solution, and often there was complete disagreement; ten, for example, saw the answer in working through Parliament and four in bypassing it. The three areas on which there was greatest agreement were an increase of pressure from outside governments on Stormont, which we have called indirect intervention, involvement of the people, and reform. In both reform and indirect intervention, reference to Q. 4 shows that people expected these would occur. Many more leaders, however, saw involvement of the people as a path to change than expected it to occur. With the balance of the political parties in a state of flux, appeals to the 'silent majority' were an attempt to build a power base from which to gain control. The fact that people on the whole did not expect this tactic to work is probably a reflection of the situation where those on both sides were prepared to take action were already doing so, as the leaders became increasingly out of touch.

As six people saw cooperation with the South and nine links with Great Britain as means to the ends, political leaders when talking about indirect intervention were referring to both of the main external forces.

BASIC PROBLEMS THAT ULSTER FACES AND POSSIBLE SOLUTIONS

Another pair of questions (9 and 10) asked the leaders to list the problems that Ulster faces and possible solutions.

There were twenty-four different issues raised, ranging from the need for parliamentary democracy to the lack of development west of the Bann. The findings show the impossibility of being able to satisfy all parties to a conflict on all issues. One person's plea for moderation stops a long way short of another's call for a revolution.

These findings also show the need for such a conflict situation to be tackled on a wide number of fronts—economic, housing, civil rights, local government reforms, long term planning and so on. An interesting difference emerges in the answers to the first four questions and Qs. 9 and 10. The former group asked subjects what they would like or expect to see happen in the future—in their answers they frequently mentioned changes in the structure of the political parties. Yet in the two questions about the problems facing Ulster, apart from four saying there was a need for parliamentary democracy, political parties did not emerge as an issue. This again suggests that people perceived that events inside the Ulster parliamentary political structure were not going materially to affect what could be done.

The three most frequently mentioned problem areas were community relations, housing and economic development. For each a variety of suggested solutions were given. There were twenty-six different remedies for the problem of community relations, eleven for housing and eighteen for the economic situation. The second point is that none of the alternatives had overwhelming support—each having one or two advocates. When these findings are combined with the answers to Q. 4, not only did people see things improving in the future but they also saw a whole variety of ways in which the problems could be solved. Compared with the answers to Q. 5, which asked for ways to achieve the leaders' aims, the present solutions are very much more specific. When looking at Q. 3, which asked about what people would like to see happen, we saw in the answers a picture of a different Ireland, where there was increased cooperation between North and South, where Catholics played a much larger part in the running of affairs in the North, where there was a viable parliamentary system under a new leader and substantial reforms had taken place. In order to be able to bring this about a need was seen for indirect intervention, economic, social and political reform and involvement of the people. In contrast the problems raised in Qs. 9 and 10 are the stepping stones which will have to be cleared away before this dream can be fulfilled. The leaders see the solution of these problems to be very much in Ulster's hands.

Ironically, most of the suggestions given here would involve Parliament in passing legislation, or at least taking positive action.

Thus the suggestions for the improvement of community relations include—integration of education, the granting of civil rights, local government reform and education of the people by Parliament. Under housing the suggestions include point allocation, housing trusts, and new town commissions. Finally, solutions to the economic problem include an industrial training programme and investment west of the Bann. The irony is that, as we have seen, political power in the short term has moved away from Parliament. It is probably because of this stalemate that there has been the emphasis (Q. 5) on the need for indirect intervention.

OUTSIDE INTERVENTION

Subjects were asked from whom this intervention might come. The span of answers, ranging from Communists to the U.S.A. Irish, indicates how people in an intercommunal situation see outside groups being involved in their affairs. Part of the reason for this comes from the situation that we have been outlining—participants do not feel that the conflict can be solved to their satisfaction by the structures that at present exist within Ulster. They therefore have to look outside; this spillover effect, as Chapter 3 discussed, is a feature of such conflicts.

The Communists are said to want to interfere in Ulster because they require a 'base from which to invade the U.S.' and they will achieve this when the situation becomes tense by taking over control of the Civil Rights Association and the IRA. When people believe things like that, then to change their attitude involves more than simply trying to put the facts straight. Individuals and groups often need to exaggerate the danger posed by the enemy in order to justify their own actions. (This is discussed later.) The fact that the USA Irish were the outside power most frequently mentioned after Great Britain and before Eire, is explained by the large number of Irish emigrants. Their intervention is by financial support for both Catholics and Protestants and also by pressure on the British and U.S. governments.

A quarter of the sample thought that Eire might interfere because of her traditional interest and because people in the South wanted reunification. Two people stated that this would occur when civil war broke out in the North and that intervention would consist primarily of propaganda interchanges with Westminster, attempts to influence the Catholic population and, according to one person, invasion. Hillery, the Eire Foreign Minister in July and August 1969, did meet then with Michael Stewart, Britain's Foreign Secretary, and when the August 1969 troubles broke out in Londonderry there was a faction within Eire which wanted the army to intervene.[1] This same faction has led subsequently to a split in the ruling Fianna Fáil party on the attitude the South should take to the North.

One in three interviewed thought that Britain would intervene, the majority when the right wing in Ulster came to power, or when the situation became unmanageable through violence. However, only one person mentioned the sending in of troops, most saying that intervention would be indirect, with the placing of pressure on O'Neill.

These findings tie in with the expectations of the future; twice as many subjects said that they expected some form of indirect as against direct intervention. It is interesting to speculate why, when most thought that there would be trouble in the short term and that Parliament was no longer able to control the situation, so few saw a possibility of direct intervention. The answer probably lies in the fact that at this stage the civil rights campaign still appeared successful, the Government was talking about introducing reforms, and the Catholics had some faith in their own actions. From the Protestant viewpoint the move to break O'Neill was gathering steam, and when it succeeded they must have hoped that this would stop the rot. The finding also implies that people within a conflict situation are unable to assess the consequences of their actions, to predict how other parties will perceive and react to their decisions.

INTERNAL OPPOSITION

In Q. 6 we asked what risks lay in introducing changes *within* Ulster. As might be expected extremists on both sides—Protestant Unionists and the People's Democracy/Civil Rights group— were singled out as the people most likely to cause danger because demonstrations would lead to a backlash and violence from both sides. This was an accurate picture of what was to occur in the following months.

A similar question (Q. 11) asked which groups or forces inside Ulster might prevent the solution of problems. Again the Catholic and Protestant extremist organisations were singled out. In all twenty-five different groups and seven individuals were named, which again indicates the difficulty facing anybody trying to alter the *status quo*. All groups from the extreme left to the extreme right were mentioned, which shows that any measure would have met opposition from someone.

While only five mentioned the IRA as an outside party which might interfere and only two said that it would form a danger in the long term to ways of changing the situation, thirteen thought that the IRA might prevent the more immediate problems being solved. This is interesting because at the time the interviews were carried out the IRA was comparatively unimportant. A split had developed between the Green IRA, the traditionalists who wanted to eliminate the border if necessary by force, and the Red IRA who, as their title suggests, were more concerned with socialist goals and had accordingly formed housing associations and similar bodies. Evidence that at this stage the Red IRA was the more dominant group is shown by the lack of arms available to defend the Catholics in the August 1969 troubles. This has since changed.

It is also worth noting that the most frequently mentioned person or group was Paisley, who was obviously seen as both leader and symbol of the extreme Protestant position. Altogether eighteen saw Paisley as a danger, seven saw the Unionist party, and five the ruling class, in the same light. One may suspect that Paisley's rise was due in part to his assuming the gap left in the extreme Protestant position by the Unionist party being forced by Westminster to adopt a more conciliatory stance towards the Catholics. The Unionist ruling class had been able to exploit the Protestant working class by convincing them that their real enemy was the Catholic community. When the ruling class was forced to moderate its position, Paisley was quite rightly able to scream betrayal; thus the Unionists found the tables being turned on them. To the extent that Paisley was attacking the ruling class, his movement was in lart part working-class based and there must be some hope of the Protestant and Catholic working class combining, in true class style, against the common enemy, the capitalist. This is a point which has long been made by the People's Democracy spokesmen.

IDENTIFICATION OF PARTIES TO THE CONFLICT

In the last question (Q. 12) we asked the subjects who they thought were the parties to the conflict. As we said in the previous chapter, if we had taken a wider sample the answers to these questions would have served as a starting point. The most important point is that fifty-seven different individuals and groups were mentioned. Obviously only a number were concerned with each of the specific issues, but even so it shows the complexity of the situation for anyone trying to bring the parties to a conflict together round a table. In a situation like this it becomes virtually impossible to organise any mediation which requires bringing together a small number of people who can be said to be representative of all the parties to the dispute.

The number of parties also shows how difficult it must be for a body such as the Home Office to be in touch with them all, especially so since the Catholics now perceive the British Government to be in league with a Protestant Stormont which has been and still is allied to the Conservative Party. It can be argued that such a task is unrealistic, and that most of the parties anyway lie outside the parliamentary system. However, much of the action has little to do with Parliament and although one cannot perhaps be in continual contact with all groups, it is essential at least to know what each of them thinks about all the issues.

It is interesting to note that both press and television are considered parties to the conflict. This reflects the influence they have had in bringing it to the attention not only of people in Britain but also in the rest of the world. In fact four people said that the British Government intervened in Ulster because of its embarrassment at the worldwide publicity.

In the second part of this question we looked at how the leading parties (measured in terms of those most frequently mentioned) were perceived. The Nationalists come out as old-fashioned, disunited, with declining significance, Catholic, and anti-partition. This fits in with the picture of the growth of support for the Civil Rights movement which concentrated on wrongs within Ulster as its first priority rather than the removal of the border. The Civil Rights party itself was seen as a new force, which was both split and too small. The other of the frequently mentioned opposition parties, the Northern Ireland Labour Party, was perceived to be middle-of-the-road and non-sectarian but having small working-class support and little influence. The small size of each of the opposition groups on its own has been one reason for the ineffectiveness of the opposition in Stormont. The continuing fractionation is in itself a result of the frustration the opposition parties have experienced from their significant lack of success, in whatever combination, in getting Stormont to operate as a vehicle of change.

In contrast the Orange Order was seen as extremist and,

according to seven people, as influential, but by two others as having declining influence. In contrast thirteen saw the IRA as being of little or no consequence while six saw it as still a threat.

Of the individuals, O'Neill was seen as conservative and right-wing, four mentioning that they were opposed to him on personal grounds. Fitt was labelled a Catholic republican one-man party, while Paisley was seen as being extremist, loyalist and living in the past. The right-wing unionists were similarly seen as reactionary.

Finally the Unionist Party was seen to be Protestant, comprehensive, split and behind the times. This description sums up many of the problems from which the Unionist party suffers. It is Protestant in so far as it has been said in the past that a vote against Unionism is a vote towards the abolition of Ulster. Yet at the same time it has tried to be comprehensive enough to cover all shades of Protestant opinion and, so some Unionists said to us, broad enough to include Catholics. Because it has tried to be comprehensive it has split under attack and has become, as both O'Neill and Chichester-Clark found out to their cost, a captive of its right wing.

BACKGROUND TO THE CONFLICT

In Chapter 2 we provided an outsider's historical outline of events leading to the present trouble. History, as we know, is dependent on the ways different people collect and organise the same available body of data. In Q. 7 we asked the subjects to indicate what they saw as the critical points in Ulster's history. Over thirty-five different points were mentioned, and of these on only one (unfair treatment of the Catholic minority) did more than ten people agree. Therefore different people had completely contrasting pictures of what has led to the present situation.

SUMMARY OF ISSUES

By looking at all the issues within each of the questions we can begin to grasp the complexity of a conflict such as Ulster's. There is no one cause, no single problem whose solution will bring an end, no agreed path to follow. Instead there are a wide variety of parties with differing views on each of the many issues. In terms of the Ulster conflict people were pessimistic about the short term but saw eventual improvement when immediate problems were solved. One major difficulty was to find a move from the present deadlock, where people had lost faith in Parliament as a viable governing unit but had not yet found any other way of implementing change. As a way out of this many parties were looking for some form of indirect intervention to act as an instigator.

THE DISPUTES

The next step is to see if any of these issues is more important than the others. Are there any underlying factors or disputes as we labelled them in the framework developed in the last chapter, which explain the pattern of issues we have just examined? As explained in Chapter 5, the most practical way in this case of identifying the disputes was to choose the issues most frequently mentioned. (These are given in the lefthand column in the results in Appendix 2.) We also used a second method of determining disputes, which was to correlate every issue with every other issue in the same question. There were, however, very few significant correlations and those that were at all meaningful were concerned with the problems people perceived to be facing Ulster. (These are given in Appendix 3.) Most of this section of the analysis is therefore based on the definition of disputes in terms of the most often mentioned issues. As many of the issues occur in more than one question, it makes it easier to follow if they are regrouped under different headings.

(a) *Short term problems.* Reform, parliamentary legitimacy, trouble on the streets, backlash, stern measures.
(b) *Underlying problems.* Reform, socio-economic, local government, implementation of five point programme, opposition growth, religion, unionist disunity, unemployment, housing, community relations, unfair treatment of Catholic minority.
(c) *Means of solving the problems.* Mobilisation of the people, indirect intervention, civil rights, integration of education.
(d) *Main dangers to change.* Paisley, IRA and the Orange Order.
(e) *Outside countries involved.* Eire, USA Irish, Great Britain.

It now becomes possible to look at each group of issues in turn and see what has been done to solve them. In the short term—the three months or so after the interviews, leading up to but not including the Apprentice Boys March of August 1969—there was little reform, more on-the-street trouble, a build-up Protestant backlash, and the retention of stern measures. As we have pointed out, time was too short for anything constructive to be done and by then events had almost achieved a momentum of their own and were probably beyond the control of those in Stormont.

If we now consider the underlying problems steps appear to have been taken, at least superficially—a Bill to introduce a central housing authority has been announced, 'one man one vote' has been granted and an Ombudsman and a Community Relations Officer have been appointed. Nearly all these steps were suggested by the subjects in the answers presented earlier. On closer examination, very little has been achieved. There is no certainty that the central housing authority Bill will pass through Parliament when it gets there later in the year. Local government reform, and thus the effect of 'one man one vote', have been delayed and the latter cannot now appear before 1972. A five-year plan for housing is a rather remote carrot to those now in need and there is little evidence that either the Ombudsman or the Minister of Community Relations is having a significant calming effect. In the meantime unemployment continues to rise and while the troubles continue foreign firms are afraid to invest. Religion retains its hold and with police and army raids in Catholic strongholds, the perceived unfair treatment of the Catholic minority has not yet ended. Therefore very little has been done to solve any of the underlying problems. The correlational approach to the disputes showed that community relations were perceived to be significantly related to unemployment and civil rights to housing. This indicates that until constructive steps are taken it seems unlikely that there will be any progress in relations between the two communities and therefore in bringing an end to the troubles.

If we look at the means the participants themselves suggested for breaking the conflict, little has been done to implement civil rights and nothing to integrate the educational system. The people have become involved to a limited extent, but it seems for negative rather than positive ends. There is much evidence that there is a continuing growth of grass-roots support for the right-wing Unionists. Similarly events like the 1969 siege of Bogside might mobilise and involve those caught inside, but this can do little to break down sectarian barriers. It may simply be because there has so far been no effective opposition party worth voting for, or it may be that those in the centre stay unmoved simply because they are by definition moderates.

An important step was the direct intervention of the British

Army. At first it was hailed with joy by the Catholics, who saw it primarily as a means of breaking the deadlock. In fact, as they failed to see at the time, it simply meant that no reforms were going to be implemented. Until then the newly found Catholic weapon of civil rights had seemed to be pushing Stormont towards granting them. The arrival of the British Army however changed the emphasis of the dispute into one of law and order, the very *status quo* against which the Catholics had been protesting. It became a question of law and order because the Catholic civil rights tactic of demonstration was now turned against the British Army instead of the 'B' Specials and RUC, the agents of the Stormont Government who became invisible behind the Army. An attack against the RUC could be presented as an attack on the social policies of the Government: but an attack on the neutral British Army was an act against law and order that could only be committed by the lunatic fringe. At the same time Stormont has followed a go-slow policy on reform in order to protect itself from the growth of Protestant right-wing opinion. Any protest was now seen as extremism. Therefore the arrival of the British troops has so far served to slow down the promised pace of reform. It has in fact taken the pressure of the protest march off Stormont's back and replaced it with the old school hand of the Westminster word. Thus the British direct intervention, at one time a possible way out of the impasse which had developed, has so far proved to be the reverse—a continuation of the *status quo* which created the problem in the first place.

If we now look at what the leaders perceived as the obstacles to reform, three parties stand out—Paisley, the IRA and the Orange Order. Paisley has continued to grow in importance and since this study was undertaken has won seats to both the Stormont and Westminster Parliaments. As we have said, he now fills the gap on the Protestant right left vacant when pressure forced the ruling Unionists at least to give the appearance of accommodating civil rights. Even though the Civil Rights campaigners predicted that the conflict would be more polarised by their actions, they could hardly have been expecting the Protestant extremists to become more firmly entrenched. This has meant that there is no longer the same need for the Protestants to protest in the streets. They still have a voice where they believe it matters. The Catholics can only communicate by demonstrating, and as we have seen the arrival of the British troops has distorted the situation.

This is one of the reasons for the return of the Green IRA. Looking back it is possible to see that the Catholics have made

K

a number of attempts to try and influence events in Ulster. They
started by not recognising the state and refusing to take seats in
Stormont. They next attempted a reign of terror through the
IRA. By the end of 1950 these tactics had obviously failed and
Catholic hopes became pinned on parliamentary representation
at Westminster and Stormont. This too failed to produce results.
Then came the civil rights demonstrations which, until the British
intervened, seemed to be working. When this activity too was
blocked it is no wonder that in frustration many people returned
to one of the previous strategies. In the meantime the fiasco of
the Londonderry and Belfast troubles of 1969, when the IRA was
patently exposed as being unable to protect the Catholic population, produced splits in the movement. The old hands, the Green
IRA, set out to make sure that next time the situation arose they
would be prepared. As the newspapers have frequently reported,
and as the British Army found to their cost, they started to rearm.
What is interesting, though, is that more subjects saw the IRA
as a finished rather than a potent force. The fact that it arose
again in its traditional form is another consequence of British
intervention and the subsequent loss of faith in it by the Catholics
as a prime mover of change.

As was pointed out in Chapter 2, the Orange Order is still a
potent force in Ulster affairs and subjects we interviewed en-
dorsed this point of view. Further evidence for this comes from
the Order's resistance to a voluntary discontinuance of marching
on 12 August 1970, and the reluctance of the Stormont and
Westminster governments to oppose them.

Among possible interventionists, Great Britain has been discussed. The Communists are only included because some of the
Ulster leaders saw the whole student protest movement, of
which People's Democracy was a part, as a worldwide Communist plot. We found no evidence of this. The American Irish
gave financial support to both sides and representatives from
many of the Ulster parties have been to the United States on
fund-raising tours.

In Eire the ruling Fianna Fáil party has been in a very difficult
position to which the British press in particular has not been
particularly sympathetic. They have given frequent warnings to
Jack Lynch not to deviate from his moderate stand without always
realising the pressures he has faced. These first came to a head in
August 1969.[1] The Foreign Minister had paid a number of visits
to London to warn the British Government of the dangers and
to ask them to intervene. They told him that it was none of
Eire's business, and that anyway the matter was well in hand.

When the disturbances broke out on the 12th the Eire Cabinet was in deep Ttrouble. hey could not afford to do nothing, as this would have played into the hands of the extremists; they could not in reality invade except as a means of drawing attention, as Eire's best troops were in Cyprus on U.N. duties. Their tactics, therefore, were aimed at forcing Britain to intervene, and this lay behind their raising the matter at the United Nations. The opening of field hospitals at the border was to show that the Government was doing something positive, and they took this action while realising that it could lead to Protestant fears of an invasion and an intensification of attacks on Catholics. The tactics proved successful and Lynch was able to maintain his policy against the elimination of the border by force and his taking no action which would upset the situation in the North. However, he could only continue this policy if it could be shown that the lot of the Catholics in the North was beginning to improve. This did not take place and what happened appeared to indicate a swing of power to the extreme Protestants. The charge could then be levelled against Lynch that he was letting down his Catholic brethren. This led to the split in the Fianna Fáil party between the hardliners who wanted more positive action to be taken and Lynch's moderates.

In looking at the more important variables, the disputes that make up the conflict, a picture emerges which begins to show why no way out of the conflict has yet materialised. The introduction of British troops, instead of being the intervention which would initiate change, turned out an ally of the *status quo* and therefore none of the basic problems have yet been tackled.

OFFICIAL PARTIES TO THE DISPUTE

Appendix 2, in addition to listing the disputes, also shows the attitudes to them of each of the main groups of political leaders that we interviewed. Ideally this analysis should have been carried out at the individual level but in order to do this effectively it would have been necessary to identify the subjects; to get round this we have had to group the individual parties in terms of the overt splits which existed at the time of the interviews.

(a) Short term problems

As might be expected it was the Established Opposition (EO)

and the Civil Rights groups (CR) who wanted and expected at least limited reform. The pro-O'Neill Unionists (PNU) and intercommunal parties (ICP) both wanted limited reform but fewer of them expected it. The Anti-O'Niell Unionists (ANU) neither expected nor wanted any reform. (The Southern Irish (SI) answers should be ignored in Qs. 1 and 2 as they were obtained six months after the other set and would therefore have been considering a different three-month period.)

The PNU were the group who wanted both the restoration of Parliament's position and a return to trouble-free conditions or what they called normality. While the *status quo* would protect the PNU's position, neither of the more extreme groups felt that it was much use. Only two of the CR group wanted a return to parliamentary action, and none wanted a return to normality. Parliament had achieved nothing for them and while civil rights protests appeared to be working, normality or lack of trouble would have been a form of surrender. The same was true for the ANU because normality meant the gradual erosion of Protestant domination.

All groups expected trouble on the streets. The two Catholic groups, EO and CR, expected this to lead to more stern measures. Even so they were prepared to continue with this tactic. For Stormont to meet force with force is not necessarily the most astute strategy. It is this resistance to change which helps to perpetuate conflicts.

(b) Underlying problems

All the groups agree on the basic problems—unemployment, housing and community relations—which face Ulster, with the single exception of the ANU who did not believe that community relations were a basic problem. This is at least one area where a common consensus could have provided a starting point for political cooperation. Given this agreement, it is not surprising that all groups also wanted socio-economic reform, and both the Unionist groups and the EO believed that this would come about. The CR were more pessimistic. In terms of overall reform, while the Unionists wanted limited reform the three Catholic groups, in particular the CR and SI advocated a larger scale of reform. The EO were by far the most optimistic that limited reform would come about. This difference between limited and large reform between Protestants and Catholics points to a danger which exists in an unbalanced conflict. The side with most holdings feels that anything it gives away is a large offer while the deprived groups, whose expectations tend to escalate rapidly on the basis of any success, are likely to spurn such an offer as paltry (see Chapter 3). Something of this state of affairs exists at present in Ulster where the Protestants feel that they have already given away too much, hence the support for Paisley, while the Catholics are being forced by the presence of the British Army to accept a very meagre token of reform.

(c) Means of solving problems

Here a clear split emerged between the Protestant and Catholic factions. While PNU and ANU emphasised the need for socio-economic reform, the Catholic groups had a three-point programme of civil rights, involvement of the people, and indirect intervention. Therefore the Catholics expected that British intervention might help the path of reform—but, as we have seen, the reverse happened. There is little use in involving the people when the enemy has retreated behind the British Army. Small wonder that the Catholics who at first welcomed the British troops should eventually turn against them. As unemployment continues to rise and with the slow-down in the growth of the British economy any hopes of socio-economic reforms working in the immediate future must be receding.

(d) Main dangers to change

The figures show clearly that the Catholics, in particular the CR, expected that their demonstrations would lead to violence and a backlash from the Protestant Unionists. Because of this, three of the EO saw the CR as a danger. This shows the split in the opposition ranks between those who had joined the civil rights movement in spirit, if not always in action, and those who preferred to work through parliamentary processes. In addition, the CR in particular saw the Orange Order and Paisley as forces who might prevent the problems being solved. In contrast, people from all groups saw the IRA as a possible danger, in particular the EO and ANU.

At first this appears to contradict the descriptions that subjects gave to parties in the conflict where two of the PNU and ANU saw the IRA as still posing a threat, while the other groups tended to see them as being of little or no consequence. The explanation is that while the Protestants saw the danger of the IRA as being that they already dominated the civil rights movement, the Catholic fears were that they might do so.

(e) Outside countries

The most striking point is that while only one in ten of the Protestant leaders expected Britain to intervene, three in four of the CR and EO groupings did. The Protestants realised that any further intervention by Britain must be in the line of diluting the powers of Stormont and furthering the civil rights campaign. Similarly it is the Catholic groups who have the highest expectations of the American Irish and Eire playing a part in Ulster's politics. This tends to show the isolation the Protestants must have felt. Westminster, especially under the Labour Government, was no longer a trusted ally; Eire was sending troops to the border; there was a resurgence in IRA activity; the 'B' Specials had been disbanded and the RUC disarmed. Fears of a big power solution being imposed with the tables reversed and Ulster becoming a Protestant enclave in hostile Catholic territory, must have contributed to the sudden movement, that for a while came into being, towards a unilateral declaration of independence. It is little wonder that Paisley, and more recently Craig and West, have been able to attract followers by talking of the need for loyal Protestants to defend themselves and to be given the necessary men and weapons.

In keeping with this beleaguered, isolationist image, are the findings which show that the majority of the ANU believed either that no one would interfere, or that it would be the Communists who did.

Looking at the ways in which the different groupings perceive the conflict, we have seen that in most cases Protestants and Catholics had a very different view of the situation. Even where they agreed, for example, on the basic problems, they disagreed on the most appropriate methods of solution.

As we said in Chapter 5, this approach towards official groupings tends to emphasise differences between them, which can be put into proportion if we look at the way the individuals group around each of the issues. Because of identification problems it was not possible to do this, but as a substitute measure we have taken one member from each group and shown how they stand in relation to the various issues as a means of demonstrating the feasibility of this approach.

PARTIES TO THE ISSUES

There were many issues on which none of the five randomly

chosen subjects expressed any opinion, there were others on which only one commented. The Pro-O'Neill Unionist, for example, was the only one who wanted to see Unionist reform in the long term. To illustrate the changing pattern of views, we have taken the ANU subject:

ANU similar

ANU/PNU—both in the short term want trouble to move off the streets.
ANU/EO—both see unemployment as a basic problem.
ANU/ICP—both see housing as a basic problem.
ANU/CR—both expect trouble on the streets in the short term.
ANU/SI—did not agree on anything.

ANU opposed

ʃANU—see street politicians as the danger to reform.
ʅPNU—see Nationalist/Republicans as the danger.
ʃANU—want no reform in the short term.
ʅEO—want limited reform in the same period.
ʃANU—want stern measures in the long term.
ʅICP—want a reduction of sternness in the long term.
ʃANU—sees improved transport as a means to solve the problems.
ʅCR—sees the granting of civil rights as the solution.
ʃANU—wants increased Unionist unity.
ʅSI—wants increased Unionist disunity.

Not only do individuals agree on some issues and disagree on others, but their grouping varies from issue to issue. If we take the three basic problems of unemployment, housing and civil rights, unemployment is seen as a problem by the EO, ANU, and ICP subjects; housing by the ANU and ICP and civil rights by the ICP and CR.

This section, therefore, shows that the more a conflict can be divided into its basic issues and groupings, not only is the complexity increased but this same complexity shows there is often much more agreement than would appear by an examination of the positions of the main official groupings. It also indicates that if each issue to a conflict is taken in turn it becomes possible to identify the relevant parties to that issue and their stand on it. With this information one then can bring together people with similar attitudes to an issue and know who is likely to be in the way of its resolution.

GROUPING OF PARTIES

We grouped the parties first in terms of the individuals' overall political allegiances. Factor analysis could be used to see if the pattern of answers of all the subjects to the disputes (it was not possible to use issues as there were in most cases too few parties to a particular issue) indicated that they were grouped together in some other manner. That is, instead of taking their overt political allegiance as a basic grouping the basis would be their overall attidues towards the whole conflict.

Two factors or groupings of people resulted from this analysis. The most important issues in the first factor were the individual's political groupings, reform, expectation of long-term trouble and expectation of danger in any of the suggested means for solving the conflict. All those with similar attitudes to these issues came from the Catholic groups except for three ICP members.

The second factor was mainly concerned with trouble in the short term. On this factor seven PNU, 4 ANU, three CR, one EO and one ICP leader had similar attitudes.

These figures suggest that at the dispute level, concerned with more general issues, allegiance to political parties accounts for a lot in explaining the way people group round a dispute. But as the pattern for the second factor shows, official political allegiance covers up the fact that people from different overt groupings can have similar attitudes to the disputes in a conflict. As we saw in the last section, when issues are considered this interchange of groupings of individuals from issue to issue becomes much more varied and complex and less dependent on official allegiances.

CONCLUSION

In this chapter we have shown how the consideration of the issues and disputes that the participants perceived to make up the conflict helps to indicate why the present stalemate has been reached. The Catholics who saw the way forward through reform and through British intervention were disappointed when the entry of the British Army restored the *status quo*. The Protestants, alarmed at the Catholics' advance, feeling weaponless and isolated, have in the meantime consolidated their parliamentary position through the election of right-wing MPs and the grass-roots pressure they have been able to exert on more moderate Unionists. The way they saw out of the situation, that of socio-economic reform, has disappeared, owing to the stagnation in the English economy. People from all groups tended to feel that unless the basic problems could be tackled there was little hope of an improvement in relations between the two sides. No one saw much hope in Parliament, as then constituted, providing the necessary leadership, and the British presence, to which the Catholics in particular had looked forward as an initiator of change, failed to fulfil this expectation.

We then moved on to consider how when the conflict was broken down into basic issues it became possible to see which issues affected which people, and how alliances varied from issue to issue and did not always fall along the lines of overt political allegiance. It is this level of analysis which could be used to find a way out of the conflict. If the move to the right continues, it will produce nothing more than a temporary lull in hostilities. One remedy might be to form a number of committees to tackle different issues on which people with different political allegiances but with similar thinking on a particular issue could serve together. Another need is to make Parliament a legitimate force again, and in order to do this there must be a viable opposition. Perhaps the new Social and Democratic Labour Party will be a first step, but unless a system of proportional representation is introduced there will eventually have to be a meaningful split within the Unionist party. A viable democracy demands that the structures reflect the wishes of the main groups within the population. The conflict has to move from one about values to one of means to an end. As we have seen both groups in fact have quite similar long objectives. The emphasis must now move on to the best way of attaining them and overcoming various problems. This must be done at both the centre and at the periphery. As we have seen, power has moved away from Parliament. So it is also at the local level that problems are posed and solutions attempted —the introduction of highly skilled community development and relations officers would be a step in the right direction.

The need is to move the conflict away from a short-term violent battle arena where all forces are concerned with holding on to the *status quo,* to a longer-term perspective where the goals are roughly agreed and what matters is how they are to be achieved.

¹ 'Crises in Cabinet', *Nusight,* pp. 3–7, October 1969.

7

Some theoretical implications of the results

We are now in a position to relate the results of our survey to the outline of conflict theory described in Chapter 1. The theoretical section of that chapter can be broken down into two parts in the first of which we showed how any conflict can be reduced to its constitutent elements by the use of sets of definitions that, at the same time, pointed to further lines of enquiry and allowed for the importation of propositions from other disciplines. In that context we introduced, as an example, frustration–aggression theory. We also described how systems terminology allowed for the creation of a new language that cut across the conventional demarcation lines between the different social sciences.

In a different context, system theory is also representative of much of the material presented in the second part of that chapter. We were able to draw attention to some of the broader over-arching theories that attempt to explain total social situations. These two parts were then combined in Chapter 3 to form a theoretical picture of intercommunal conflict. This model showed how the constant changes within and across parties, and the effects of misperception based on the configuration of the social structure, could create a dangerously unstable situation that would become more violent and repressive through time. Chapter 2, in describing the background to the Ulster conflict, attempted to validate the broader outlines of this model.

In broad terms our analysis completes the justification for combining these two approaches. The complexity of the issues and parties revealed by our questionnaire validates the use of sets of distinctions and definitions to break down the complex inter-actions involved in any conflict. Limited propositions from other fields concerning such phenomena as misperception also appear to be relevant to the interviews that we obtained. On the other hand it is impossible to describe the conflict in Ulster as we did in

Chapter 2 without recognising the relevance of the overarching theories. Thus Jenkins's use of rank disequilibrium and Boserup's concentration on the major economic linkages involved, also seem relevant.

However, there is a large gap between these two levels of theory. We may use a major defect in our own analysis to make this point. Had we been able to repeat our study after a time interval, we would have been able to undertake two more processes of analysis. In the first instance we would have obtained a picture of changes in the conflict over time which would have allowed us to build more immediately predictive models which cannot at present be constructed from the type of theories available. In fact the more repeat studies that can be undertaken the better, because an inspection of the relatively stable patterns and trends in the conflict would allow us to test, in a meaningful fashion, for the existence of the structures and processes postulated by overarching theory. In the same context one could see how the broad structural features of a society have their effect in particular times and places. This last point is best illustrated by an example.

Let us make a more careful inspection of a macro-theory such as rank disequilibrium theory; which as we saw in Chapter 1 forms a major part of Galtung's approach. We can say that the necessary ingredients of rank imbalance theories are, first, the stratification of members of the investigated social entity according to at least two different criteria (e.g. income and colour of skin); each criterion should have at least the properties of an ordinal scale. That is to say, we should be able to say accurately that X is richer than Y. Secondly, the theory assumes that different psychological states will be the result of different positions on the two scales for any one individual. We should, for example, have some assumptions about whether or not a particular combination will make a person happy or sad or frustrated. Lastly, we must make some assumptions about the likely response of individuals to their emotional state. We might expect a person caught in a particular imbalance situation to be more prone to suicide, or less inclined to save money than other people.

Given those ingredients, the substance of this theory is that individuals having the same relative positions on all the status dimensions will behave differently from individuals not having such a consistent or congruent status profile. They will experience psychological tension because 'persons with a low degree of status congruence are more likely to be subjected to disturbing experiences in the interaction process and have greater difficulty in establishing rewarding patterns of social interaction than others'.[1] The reader will be reminded here of the description given earlier of the difficulties faced by aspiring middle-class Catholics and poor Protestants in Northern Ireland.

Such theories have been widely applied to problems connected with small groups, national societies, and even to interstate relations. In all cases the research results are ambiguous and the correlations are low. Many sets of results using the same data are contradictory. Yet as is so often the case social scientists claim that very low correlations must be expected because of the complexity of the social field understudy. However, such an explanation goes only so far. In this context Zelditch and Anderson[1] have provided a critical analysis of status incongruence theories which is helpful in pointing to the difficulties which we suggest exist with the exclusive use of this broad type of theory.

The first of these is that the analyst using such theories has to make an initial decision as to what are the relevant value dimensions in a society, always bearing in mind that they will not necessarily be the same for all individuals. Out of a multitude of dimensions, we can only establish the relative importance of the two that are chosen by investigating their subjectively perceived importance. This points to the need for a great deal of pilot work. For example in one survey it was found that family structure rather than wealth may be a more important determining factor in the abilities of families to save.

Once we have established the importance of the dimensions, we must next establish their salience (or relevance to the people concerned) and examine the manner in which they are mediated by local community norms and patterns of behaviour. For example, it has been pointed out that a relatively wealthy Negro doctor may be affected by status incongruence if he works in a white area, but not if he works in a Negro area. Even having established both the importance and salience of a dimension, we have to be sure whether the sample have consonant perceptions of what constitutes any particular dimension. Do people, for example, have similar conceptions of who is rich and who is poor?

These problems indicate that an enormous amount of information is required before such a theory could be satisfactorily tested over large numbers of people. However it may be suggested that there is still some validity in the theory because correlations are occasionally found in certain circumstances, but 'to suggest that where there is such a correlation it is an exemplification of some general law of incongruence is not to bring explanation nearer but rather to defer it, as the true explanation will be found in "those certain circumstances" in which some criteria of differential treatment are seen as relevant rather than others, and some comparative reference groups obtrude themselves rather than others out of a range of possibilities which cannot all be subsumed under one covering hypothesis.'[1]

The point is that macro-theoretical propositions require a great deal of testing so that the effects of local mediating factors can be worked out. Otherwise large-scale theories remain clothed in self-fulfilling armour. On the other hand, micro-level research, concerned with limited areas or groups of people, only allows for the making of trivial predictions. The framework outlined in this book attempts to provide an intermediate level in which the basic issues and parties dealt with at micro-level can be grouped together to provide a comprehensive view of the conflict that should relate to macro-theoretical propositions as well.

Macro-theory (for example, stratification theory) tends to deal with very broad configurations of society, such as the distribution of capital and classes. Such relationships are slow-moving and affect immediate behaviour only by circuitous paths. A knowledge of the relationship between capital and class is not of much use when attempting to predict events in the next six months, or its categories are so vague that almost any social change will fit the theory. Again, the restrictions of our survey, especially the fact that it had to be cross-sectional, prevented us from undertaking any predictions, so it is only a hypothesis that more effective prediction will be obtained from this level of analysis. We return to this later in this chapter.

It is legitimate to ask, in the light of the above comments, why we saw fit to publish at this stage. There are two reasons. The first is that the end of this project marked a natural point at which to attempt to gain the widest possible reaction to our ideas before developing them further. The second is that the use of this technique raises grave ethical problems. There are two broad schools of thought about the nature of social conflict. One of them regards conflict as a disease of society that interrupts its normal workings. The opposite view is that conflict is a reflection of the social structure and processes. The corollary of this latter view is that the resolution of social conflict must imply the restructuring of the society concerned. Obviously, any theory that yields a significant amount of prediction and control will have profound effects for the society. This is obviously not yet a problem that affects us here (though the issues remain in principle). What does affect us here is another of the implications of our research.

Our inclination is to view conflict as the direct output of the social structure. Even the very limited sample used here indicated that the conflict occupied a large part of the respondent's life-space, from what they ate and where they lived, through their religion and standard of living, to their views on the future of their country. If conflict resolution *is* the long-term aim of conflict research, then it follows that resolution in such areas as this will rely on detailed knowledge of local social patterns; the sort of knowledge that is derived from survey data. The possession of such knowledge creates problems. Fortunately maybe, our data are too sparse to be of much use, but a larger survey could easily act as a policeman's guide to the whereabouts and aims of local troublemakers. Clearly 'publish and be damned' is not a suitable password for the researcher who has information that the different parties have different opportunities to make use of. And if he is to become involved in the situation, for whom is he resolving the conflict? What sort of social restructuring does he envisage? And if he is merely making it possible for the parties to the conflict to restructure their environment, then we must ask which parties will benefit by it and at whose expense? Again, the sort of methods envisaged in controlled communication rely fundamentally on introducing a reperception of social relationships that include a sensitivity and concern for the aims of opponents; but if analysis shows that the number of parties involved is larger than three or four, each with complex and shifting memberships, the problems associated with introducing learning and sensitivity are enormous.

The crux of the matter is that conflict involves change, and change involves the distribution of rewards in a society. If the analyst wishes to involve himself in that process he has then to face the responsibilities associated with it. These problems may not be only questions of principle, but immediate dilemmas. To illustrate this, we take up again our discussion of the practical output of our type of analysis and attempt to demonstrate the sort of programmes of conflict resolution that can be based on this intermediate level type of research. In view of the state of our research these suggestions will be very tentative.

We start by inquiring how local leaders are capable of introducing change at the local level. First, because of the allegiance they command, they are capable of manipulating sanctions. Secondly, they have a certain amount of knowledge concerning their constituents and their attitudes. This gives them, thirdly, the limited ability to predict the likely outcome of their actions. Thus, for example, a local leader in Belfast could polarise the situation considerably by spending time going round communally mixed housing estates frightening members of his own community with stories of imminent attack from the opposite community. This same leader could command sufficient resources to offer to move out his constituents. Many of the people he talked with could hardly afford not to believe him because of their need to protect their property and their famlies. If this process was repeated on three or four more housing estates in town, then that community would have become significantly more polarised.

Let us suppose that some party wanted to reverse this process. Add the further condition that this party had none of the sanctions that flow from local leadership and patronage networks. He would have to rely on superior information. He would have a much increased chance of success if he was aware of the attitudes of a vast number of the people concerned. He might even be able to appeal to different attitudes and images located in the constituents of the local leader. An analogy here is two market research companies trying to penetrate the same market for two products.

This idea would need to be based on several conditions before it could in principle be presented as a method of creating social change. It rests on the condition that there is some fluidity in the attitudes and images current in a society. There must be the possibility of the community developing in more than one way. Can different groupings of people and different political programmes be shaped out of the same material that supported another social order? In the last chapter we demonstrated that when a conflict is reduced to its basic elements, one can regroup sets of people into different coalitions *according to their own ideas*. Of course the difference between people regrouping their own ideas and an analyst doing it theoretically for them is tremendous. To state that a community always presents alternatives to itself in this way would be tendentious. All that we maintain is that the large amount of computing power afforded by modern machines allows one to investigate alternatives in this fashion. Furthermore, we would hypothesise that in times of conflict and change, alternate patterns would be found. (Already there is a problem that we only note for the time being; that it would be difficult to see whether or not the alternatives were, in any way, superior or inferior to the present state of things.)

The next problem that we come to is concerned with the whole nature of social change. To take an example, the Marxists' objection to the technique we are outlining would be that it consists of a mere tinkering with the superstructure of society. So long as the superstructure is determined by the deeper sub-structure of economic forces, efforts to create change at the superstructural level are doomed to failure. This may be the case. Certainly the authors would not presume to advocate any particular position in this debate. We can only mention several possibilities. The first is that the so called substructure and superstructure may be in an interactive relationship. The second is that the substructure may be equally multideterminate. The last is that superstructural change may be speeded in the direction of substructural change. For example, the analysis at the end of Chapter 2 indicates the possibility of Ulster splitting along class lines. If this was the case, superstructural change might make the process less costly for all the groups concerned. This brings us back to fundamental issues concerning the nature of conflict. If one views conflict as the result of resistance to social change, then an easing of social change in the 'right' direction would be a 'correct' act.

We should again emphasise that these are problems for the future. At present the social sciences are a haven for disillusioned refugees from the physical sciences and their heavy responsibilities for damage to the human environment. However, the possibility of a social science that works are, it seems to us, twice as daunting. Even at the immediate stage, the information collected by survey methods is of value to some groups in society and can cause alarm to others. It is a weak excuse for an economist hired by a government to say that the latest deflationary measures and the effect that they have had on living standards are the responsibility of the government, and that he had nothing to do with them.

To be frank, we had hardly considered the problem of the values concerned in this sort of research when we started the project. However, looking at the field of conflict research, one can see various positions already being taken up. J. W. Burton's technique of controlled communication is based on the notion that new solutions are generated by the parties themselves— the panel only acts in providing new concepts and a neutral supportive audience. This is fine so long as the people round the table have the trust of their communities and the necessary control flowing from that trust. After the exercise is finished events will change in the affected area in a way that they would not if the exercise had not taken place. Surely there is some responsibility here.

Considerations such as this seem to have influenced another school of structuralists led by Galtung, who seeing the need for total social reform in conflict situations, seemed prepared to take direct action in the field, possibly through some of the parties concerned. This school faces the responsibility involved in equating peace with social justice; in effect, taking up a political stance. There is yet another school who insist that, given the vast imperfections of the theory and techniques at our disposal, the subject should remain academic until the issues have been more carefully explored.

To sum up, it is our contention that detailed field work is necessary to provide the missing link between isolated micro-level studies and overarching theory. We see the possibility that research of this order could provide effective tools for resolving conflict and creating social change. This possibility means that behavioural science must weigh the responsibilities that come with social power. Consequently, the design and execution of research must be preceded by an examination of the values implicit in the research and its likely consequences.

[1] This section relies heavily on Ole Jess Olsen, 'Some comments on the theories of status incongruence', Institute for Peace and Conflict Research, No. 4, February 1970.

L

Appendix 1

Basic Issues

Question 1: As regards the political situation what would you like to see happen in Ulster in the next three months?

Intervention[1]	*Non-intervention by G.B.*[2]	*Non-intervention by Eire*
2	2	3

Stern measures[3]	*No stern measures*[4]
8	4

No reform[5]	*Limited reform*[6]	*Large reform*[7]
3	23	13

Increased Unionist unity[8]	*Increased Unionist disunity*[9]	*Increased Opposition unity*[10]
5	5	5

Increased Opposition disunity
1

Revolution Civil War	*On street trouble*[11]	*Peaceful demonstrations*[12]	*Off streets*[13]	*Normalcy*[14]
0	3	1	7	11

Parliamentary legitimacy[15]	*Parliamentary illegitimacy*[16]
17	2

Increased Civil Rights support	*Decreased Civil Rights support*
2	—

Support partition	*Anti-partition*[20]	*Increased Catholic participation*[21]	*No increased Catholic participation*
1	3	6	—

Mobilisation of the people[17]	*Don't know*	*Time too short*[19]	*Unionist reform*	*An election*
7	1	3	3	2

Backlash[18]

0

Change of Prime Minister No change in Prime Minister

6 — —

Pro-O'Neill Anti-O'Neill Established Opposition CR/PD
Unionist Unionist

11 9 12 11

Intercommunal parties Southern Irish
6 15

Questions 1 and 2

Explanations of categories; examples of answers coded in different categories

1 'Stormont abolished direct rule from Westminster' and 'we must stay back and see whether the British Government makes sure that reforms are implemented'.

2 'End of British rule in the six counties.'

3 'At present there is too much appeasement.'

4 This category was defined as wanting to drop the Special Powers Act.

5 'I don't believe it is time for the Unionist Government to make concessions.'

6 This refers to the implementation of the Government's limited reforms programme. 'It should satisfy all reasonably based demands.'

7 Where more than the Government's planned reform programme was demanded.

8 'The Unionist party should be more closely knit together.'

9 'The Unionist party would be easier to fight if the right wing element took over.'

10 'The emergence of a credible opposition in Parliament.'

11 'Need to mount more effective street demonstrations.'

12 'The pressure will be kept up.'

13 'Like to see Civil Rights marches desisting.'

14 'A period of calm and acceptance.'

15 People who would like to see change come about via Parliamentary action (e.g. 'Parliament must settle down and legislate.')

16 'Normal parliamentary opposition cannot accelerate the implementation of fundamental Civil Rights.'
17 'Mobilise public opinion to discredit people in the streets.'
18 'This will give Paisley's crowd an excuse for counterdemonstrating.'
19 'Short term doesn't appeal too much.'
20 'Want to see the reunification of Ireland.'
21 'Protestants and Catholics uniting on real issues.'

Question 2: Now speaking realistically what do you actually expect will happen in Ulster in the next three months?

Intervention	Non-intervention by GB	Non-intervention by Eire
2	1	0

Stern measures	No stern measures
12	1

No reform	Limited reform	Large reform
7	20	1

Increased Unionist unity	Increased Unionist disunity	Increased Opposition unity
—	3	3

Increased Opposition disunity
3

Revolution Civil War	On street trouble	Peaceful demonstrations	Off streets	Normalcy
4	35	2	0	7

Parliamentary legitimacy	Parliamentary illegitimacy
1	—

Increased Civil Rights support	Decreased Civil Rights support
2	2

Mobilisation of the people	Don't know	Backlash
9	1	13

Support Partition	Anti-partition
—	2

Increased Catholic participation	No increased Catholic participation
1	1

Change of Prime Minister   *No change in Prime Minister*
    7   2

Question 3: Now considering the next five years, what developments, if any, would you like to see happen?

Direct intervention[1]   *Indirect intervention*[2]   *Non-intervention*[3]
    4   5   1

Leadership change[4]   *No leadership change*
    4   —

Stern measures   *Less stern measures*
    3   7

Limited reform	*Large reform*[5]	*Local Government reform*	*Socio-economic reform*[6]	*Education reform*[7]
12	11	11	26	3

Unionist unity	*Unionist disunity*	*Unionist reform*	*Unionist decline*
1	4	7	2

Opposition unity growth	*Extremists out*[11]	*NILP growth*	*Nationalists decline*
11	2	4	1

CR/PD growth
    1

Improved community relations	*Normalcy*	*Trouble*[8]	*Civil war*
8	2	1	1

Parliamentary legitimacy   *Parliamentary illegitimacy*[9]
    9   1

Less religion[10]   *Mobilise people*
    7   11

Anti-partition	*Cooperation with South*	*Links between GB and Ulster*[12]
11	10	7

Increased Catholic participation   *No increased Catholic participation*
    6   1

Questions 3, 4 and 5

Explanations of categories

   1 'May be necessary to revert to direct rule from Westminster.'

'I would like to see Westminster come in early rather than late, including sending in troops if necessary.'

2 This category includes references to the need for GB standards influence from GB on Westminster and tripartite agreements between GB/Eire/Stormont.

3 This includes both Eire and GB, e.g. 'no intervention from GB' and 'Southern politicians must refrain from using the border as a universal political slogan!'

4 'O'Neill out of office.'

5 Refers to all the aims of the Civil Rights movement being approved.

6 'Industrial expansion' and 'a general improvement of living standards'.

7 'It could try to pilot schemes to integrate the educational system.'

8 'I see considerable unrest which may lead to a shedding of blood.'

9 'Parliament is quite hopeless.'

10 'Would like to see the complete diminution of religious implication voting.'

11 'Separation between Unionists and the Orange Order.'

12 'Would like to see Northern Ireland as part of the UK Federal System.'

Question 4: Again, speaking realistically, what do you think will happen in Ulster over the next five years?

Direct intervention	Indirect intervention
7	14

Leadership change	No leadership change
9	1

Stern measures	Less stern measures
3	1

Limited reform	Large reform	Local government reform	No local government reform	Socio-economic reform
11	4	8	1	13

Education reform
1

Unionist disunity	Unionist reform	No Unionist reform	Unionist growth	Unionist decline
11	2	2	3	5

Opposition unity growth	Opposition disunity	Extremists out	NILP growth
11	5	1	4

CR/PD growth	CR/PD decline	Paisleyite decline	Nationalists decline
3	4	2	4

Mobilise people
8

Improved community relations	Normalcy	Trouble
5	10	13

Parliamentary legitimacy	Parliamentary illegitimacy
3	1

Less religion	More religion
11	2

Anti-partition	Accept partition	Cooperation with South	Increased Catholic participation
5	4	9	7

Links between GB and Ulster
7

Question 5 : Given what you would like to see happen in Ulster in the future, what do you think are the most effective ways to achieve these aims?

Direct intervention	Indirect intervention	non-intervention
1	16	3

Leadership change	Mobilise people
2	22

Stern measures	Less stern measures
3	1

Limited reform	Large reform	Socio-economic reform	No socio-economic reform	Education reform
10	5	14	1	7

Unionist disunity	Unionist reform	Unionist growth
4	6	1

Opposition unity growth	Extremists out	NILP growth	NILP decline
10	3	1	1

Improved community relations	Trouble	Civil war
7	6	2

Parliamentary legitimacy	Parliamentary illegitimacy
10	4

Less religion	More religion
3	1

Anti partition	Co-operation with South	Increased Catholic participation
4	6	6

Links between GB and Ulster
9

Question 6: Taking each of these ways in turn, do you think there is any danger in using any of them?

No danger	No danger but	Yes a danger
11	7	18

Who will cause danger?

Protestant Unionists	IRA	PD/CR	GB
8	2	4	2

What will cause danger?

Peaceful demonstrations	Violent demonstrations	Catholic backlash	Reform
7	8	1	3

Increased Catholic population	Underestimating power government and Orange Order	Weak government
2	1	3

Danger because of

Imprisonment	Protestant backlash	Catholic backlash	Violence	Collapse of Unionist party system
1	7	4	9	2

Question 7: Could you briefly indicate what you think are the critical points in Ulster's history which have led to the present situation?

Election of O'Neill	O'Neill's mismanagement	O'Neill's lack of person
2	6	3

O'Neill too dominant
2

Gulf between N. and S. Ireland   Eire feels N. is an occupied place
2   1

O'Neill/Lemass meeting
8

Ulster's dependence on   GB pressure   English embarrassment
mother country   *over Ulster*
1   2   1

Lack of GB concern over Ulster
1

Negative attitudes of   Ecumenical movement   Pope Paul Catholic
RC Church   *reforms*
3   1   1

Predominance of religion in Ulster
2

'B' Specials Ulster Volunteers   Paisleyism   Influence of Orange Order
3   3   7

Fears of Catholic nationalism   Unionism Ulster   Unionist IRA bogy
by Unionists
6   3   2

Protestants being discriminated against
3

Influence of International Civil   CR using violence to force Wilson's
Rights, student unrest   *hand*
6   1

CR/PD extremists   Catholic mobilisation   Advent of student
involvement   *leadership*
2   4   3

Stormont over reaction to Civil Rights
4

Special powers   Gerrymandering   Unfair treatment of Catholic minority
3   5   14

Welfare for Catholics   Poor social conditions   Partisanship of police
2   5   1

Polarised communities in Ulster	Unionist neglect of Ulster
3	3

Life here very violent/Masculine	Decline of the Nationalists
1	1

Unionism élitism/using class difference	Use of welfare to buy off RC protests
4	1

Disunited opposition	People living in the past
1	1

Influence of media
4

Question 8: Which groups or countries outside Ulster do you think might interfere in Ulster's politics and why?

Eire	IRA	GB	USA	Irish Expatriate Irish	Third World	Communist eastern bloc
13	5	22	20	8	2	9

World opinion	UN	None	West Germany	British public opinion	Sinn Fein	Everyone
4	5	9	1	1	3	1

COMMUNISTS

WHY		WHEN	HOW	
Introduce links in all countries	Base to invade US	If situation tense	Control Civil Rights	Take over IRA
1	1	1	2	1

EIRE

	WHY		WHEN
Traditional Interest	Proximity	Because people there want reunification	Civil war
3	1	6	2

HOW

Influence Catholic population	Propaganda chat to Westminster	Alliance with Stormont against PD	Invade
2	3	1	1

GREAT BRITAIN
WHY

1949 Act ultimate responsibility part of UK	*Dislike publicity about Ulster*	*Part of Commonwealth*	*Economic subsidy*
6	4	1	4
Irish MPs at Westminster	*Irish population in England*	*Effect on British industry*	*Wilson needs a boost*
1	5	1	1

GREAT BRITAIN

WHEN

Right wing in power	*Violence Civil war Unmanageable situation*
3	10

GREAT BRITAIN

HOW

Economic intervention	*Pressure on O'Neill*	*Direct legislation*	*Eject N. Ireland*	*Troops*
4	5	2	1	1

USA

Trade links	WHY *Militant angry/misguided interest Irish aims*	*Disrupt trade*	HOW *financial support*	*Pressure influence of Wilson*
2	13	1	11	8

Question 9: Could you please describe what you think are the most important problems that Ulster has to solve at the moment?

Acceptance of GB standards	*Relations with the Republic*	*Links with GB*
7	2	4
Agriculture[1]	*Lack of development west of the Bann*	*Drift from land*
4	7	3

Economic development	*Poor and rich*[2]	*Unemployment*
10	4	28

Housing	*Health and welfare*	*Education*[3]	*Sectarianism/ Community relations*[4]
21	3	5	26

Lack of RC participants	*Civil Rights*	*Lack of effective opposition*	*Need for parliamentary democracy*
2	11	2	4

Need for revolution	*Need for moderation*
1	2

Rule of law	*Local government reform*	*Need for leadership*	*Influence of Orange Order*
2	3	3	1

Existence of public order. Special Powers Act.

3

Explanation of categories
1 'Need for agricultural assistance.'
2 'Allocation of resources from rich to poor.'
3 'Need for better education.'
4 'Problem of bringing people together.'

Question 10: How do you think each of these problems is
going to be solved?

COMMUNITY RELATIONS

Education of people by Parliament	*Educational integration*	*Disappearance of Nationalist Party*	*Unionist reform*	*Paisley decline*
4	7	1	2	1

Reform of Orange Order	*Catholic participation*	*Civil Rights being granted*	*Implementation of Five-point Plan*
1	2	8	1

Introduction of a Race Relations Act	*Repeal of stern measures*	*Ombudsman*	*Joint organisations*
1	4	1	1

Local government reform	Superordinate goods	Attitude change churches	Responsible leaders
2	2	5	2

More stern measures	Legal precision	Bipartisanship	Increased participation of people in general
2	1	3	2

Government demonstrations	Get rid of class differences	Amendment of 1920 Act	Increased agitation	Increased affluence
1	2	1	1	1

HOUSING

Point allocation	Housing trusts	New town commissions
4	1	1

Catholics in house planning	Central planning	More houses
1	2	4

Local government reform	Slum clearance	Expanding economy	Government aid	Self-help
1	1	2	1	1

ECONOMIC DEVELOPMENT

Industrial investment	Making N. Ireland a development area	World trade improving	Increased employment	Adequate housing
7	1	2	1	1

Shift of population from country to town	Industrial training programme	Better agriculture	GB intervention
1	2	3	1

Central planning	Destroy Unionists	Improved transport	Tourists
1	1	1	2

Cut down road spending	Nationalisation	Invest west of Bann
1	2	6

Cultivate home market	Greater integration with Republic
1	1

Question: 11 Which people or forces in Ulster do you think might prevent these problems being solved? What motives or reasons would they have and what tactics might they use?

Nationalists	NUM	Independents	Opposition parties
4	4		2

Queen's University PD	Civil Rights	Street politicians, Socialists, Catholic Extremists, Republicans, Marxists, International communists		
2	2	9		

Orange Order	Protestant extremists	Protestant working class	UCDC	UUF
12	11	2		1

RUC	Establishment ruling class vested interests	Extreme hard core right wing Unionists hard line ANV
1	5	10

Stormont Cabinet	Unionist Party, Unionist Organisation, Unionist	Local Conservative Government
2	7	1

British Parliamentary Unionist Party	Man of the electorate
2	2

IRA	Republicans anti-partition	Black institutions Ancient Order of Hibernians	Churches	Southern Irish	Catholic hierarchy
13	3	3	2	1	3

O'Neill	Brook Taylor Brookeborough	Craig	Chichester-Clark	Simpson Boal	Bunting	Paisley
3	1	1	1	1	4	18

Press
1

Question 12: Part 1

Republican Labour	Nationalists	NDP	NILP	Liberals	Derry Labour Party	Social Democrats
11	33	8	28	13	2	1

PACE	NUM	Campaign for social justice	Ulster moderates
7	8	2	3

Queen's University PD	Civil Rights	Derry Citizens Action Committee	Street politicians, Socialists, Catholic extremists, Republicans, Marxists, International Communists
29	36	5	4

Orange Order	*Protestant extremists*	*Protestant working class*	*UCDC UUF*
15	2	3	1

RUC	*Extreme Ulster Protestant Unionists*	*Establishment ruling class vested interests*	*Extreme hard core right wing Unionist Hard line ANV*
1	5	6	18

Moderate Unionists PHU Liberal Unionists	*Stormont Cabinet*	*Unionist Party Unionist Organization Unionists*	*British Parliamentary Unionist Party*	*Senate*
15	2	34	3	2

IRA	*Republicans anti-partition*	*Black institutions Ancient Order of Hibernians*	*Churches*	*Southern Irish*	*Catholic hierarchy*
21	11	1	5	3	5

Press	*TV*	*Britain*
1	7	4

Independents	*Opposition Parties*	*Devlin (P)*	*Fitt*	*Cooper*	*Hume*
	12	3	10	11	14

Farrell	*McArthur*	*Devlin (B)*	*Boyle*	*McCann*
3	5	7	2	4

O'Neill	*Brook Taylor Brookeborough*	*Faulkner*	*Craig*
13	3	3	7

Chichester-Clark	*Orr*	*Simpson Boal*	*Bunting*	*Paisley*
3	0	1	2	25

Question 12: Part 2

NATIONALISTS

Catholic	*Antipartition*	*Disunity*	*Declining significance*	*Old-fashioned Conservative*	*Green Tories*
4	8	7	14	13	

NILP

Middle of the road non-sectarian	*Little working-class support*	*Weak, small little influence*
10	5	12

CIVIL RIGHTS

Approve	*Neutral*	*Disapprove*	*New force*	*Too small, ineffective*	*Split*
8	15	10	4	3	6

ORANGE ORDER

Extremists	Influential	Declining influence
3	7	2

IRA

Still a threat	Little or no consequence
6	13

O'NEILL

Opposed to him personally	Conservative right wing
4	4

FITT

One main party	Catholic republican anti-Unionist
2	4

HUME

Pro	Against
10	3

RIGHT-WING UNIONISTS

Support UDI	Reactionary
2	5

PAISLEY(ites)

Extremists	Living in the past	Loyalist
12	4	5

UNIONISTS

Comprehensive	Protestant	Split	Behind the times, backward-looking
9	4	11	4

Appendix 2

Disputes to the conflict and the attitudes of the formal political grouping to them

Question 1: As regards the political situation what would you like to see happen in Ulster in the next three months?

	Pro-O'Neill	Anti-O'Neill	Established opposition	Civil Rights	Inter-communal parties	Southern Irish
Limited reform	5	1	6	3	3	5
Parliamentary legitimacy	5	2	2	2	4	2
Large reform	1	0	3	3	3	3
Normalcy	6	2	0	0	1	2
	11	9	12	11	6	15

Question 2: Now speaking realistically what do you actually expect will happen in Ulster in the next three months?

	Pro-O'Neill	Anti-O'Neill	Established opposition	Civil Rights	Inter-communal parties	Southern Irish
On street trouble	6	5	7	9	4	4
Limited reform	3	1	4	5	2	5
Backlash	3	2	0	3	2	3
Stern measures	2	0	4	5	1	0
	11	9	12	11	6	15

Question 3: Now considering the next five years, what developments, if any, would you like to see happen?

	Pro-O'Neill	Anti-O'Neill	Established opposition	Civil Rights	Inter-communal parties	Southern Irish
Socio-economic reform	7	5	6	5	1	2
Limited reform	3	5	1	1	2	0
Large reform	0	0	2	5	1	3
Local government reform	0	3	3	3	2	0
Opposition unity growth	1	0	6	4	0	0
Anti-partition	1	0	2	2	0	6
Mobilise people	0	1	3	4	2	1
	11	9	12	11	6	15

Question 4: Again, speaking realistically, what do you think will happen in Ulster over the next five years?

	Pro-O'Neill	Anti-O'Neill	Established opposition	Civil Rights	Inter-communal parties	Southern Irish
Indirect intervention	2	0	2	2	2	6
Socio-economic reform	5	4	3	0	0	1
Limited reform	2	2	4	2	1	0
Unionist disunity	4	1	2	1	1	2
Opposition growth	0	2	7	1	1	0
Less religion	2	4	0	4	1	0
	11	9	12	11	6	15

Question 5: Given what you would like to see happen in Ulster in the future, what do you think are the most effective ways to achieve these aims?

	Pro-O'Neill	Anti-O'Neill	Established opposition	Civil Rights	Inter-communal parties	Southern Irish
Mobilise people	2	2	5	7	3	3
Indirect intervention	0	0	5	4	1	5
Socio-economic reform	4	4	2	1	2	1
	11	9	12	11	6	15

Question 6: Taking each of these ways in turn, do you think there is any danger in using any of them?

	Pro-O'Neill	Anti-O'Neill	Estab-lished opposition	Civil Rights	Inter-communal parties	Southern Irish
No danger	2	3	2	2	2	
No danger, but	0	5	0	2	0	
Yes, a danger	2	0	7	7	2	
WHO Protestant Unionists	0	1	4	3	0	
CR/PD	0	1	3	0	0	
WHAT Demonstra-tions	0	1	4	7	2	
WHY Violence	0	1	2	6	0	
Protestant backlash	1	0	3	3	0	
	11	9	12	11	6	15

Question 7: Could you briefly indicate what you think are the critical points in Ulster's history which have led to the present situation?

	Pro-O'Neill	Anti-O'Neill	Estab-lished opposition	Civil Rights	Inter-communal parties	Southern Irish
Unfair treat-ment to Catholic minority	2	0	0	4	0	8
	11	9	12	11	6	15

Question 8: Which groups or countries outside Ulster do you think might interfere in Ulster's politics and why?

	Pro-O'Neill	Anti-O'Neill	Established opposition	Civil Rights	Inter-communal parties	Southern Irish
Eire	1	2	4	3	3	0
Great Britain	1	1	9	8	3	0
USA Irish	2	2	5	8	3	0
Communist Eastern bloc	1	4	0	1	2	1
None	1	4	0	0	0	4
GB when violence/war out of control	1	1	5	2	1	0
	11	9	12	11	6	15

Question 9: Could you please describe what you think are the most important problems that Ulster has to solve at the moment?

	Pro-O'Neill	Anti-O'Neill	Established opposition	Civil Rights	Inter-communal parties	Southern Irish
Unemployment	6	5	6	8	3	
Housing	4	4	4	6	3	
Community relations	5	1	8	7	5	
	11	9	12	11	6	15

Question 10: How do you think each of these problems is going to be solved?

	Pro-O'Neill	Anti-O'Neill	Established opposition	Civil Rights	Inter-communal parties	Southern Irish
CR Civil Rights being granted	1	0	4	3	0	
CR Education integration	2	0	3	2	0	
Economic Industrial investment	3	1	1	1	1	
	11	9	12	11	6	15

Question 11: Which people or forces in Ulster do you think might prevent these problems being solved? What motives or reasons would they have and what tactics might they use?

	Pro-O'Neill	Anti-O'Neill	Established opposition	Civil Rights	Inter-communal parties	Southern Irish
Paisley	5	0	3	7	3	
IRA	2	3	4	2	2	
Orange order	0	0	1	7	3	
	11	9	12	11	6	15

Question 12 : Part 2

	Pro-O'Neill	Anti-O'Neill	Established opposition	Civil Rights	Inter-communal parties	Southern Irish
Nationalists declining significance	2	3	2	1	2	4
Nationalists old-fashioned	3	2	2	2	1	3
NILP little influence	2	3	3	1	3	0
Civil Rights disapprove	4	4	0	1	0	0
IRA little or no consequence	0	1	3	2	2	5
IRA still a threat	2	2	0	0	0	0
Paisleyites extremists	2	1	3	3	1	2
Unionists split	2	1	2	2	2	2
	11	9	12	11	6	15

Appendix 3

Disputes determined by the inter-correlation of issues

o indicates number of interviewees not mentioning this as an issue
1 indicates number of interviewees mentioning this as an issue

Question 9:

	9 Housing		
	o	1	
5 Lack of development			
o	41	16	57
1	2	5	7
Total	43	21	64

Chi-Square value 5·32
Degree of Freedom 1 significant at 0·05 per cent level

	9 Housing		
	o	1	
8 Unemployment			
o	33	3	36
1	10	18	28
Total	43	21	64

Chi-Square Value 22·37
Degree of Freedom 1 significant at 0·01 per cent level

	23 Sectarianism/community relations		
	o	1	
8 Unemployment			
o	27	9	36
1	12	16	28
Total	39	25	64

Chi-Square Value 6·84
Degree of Freedom 1 significant at 0·01 per cent level

		14	Civil Rights	
9 Housing		0	1	
	0	39	4	43
	1	14	7	21
Total		53	11	64

Chi-Square value 5·72
Degree of Freedom 1 significant at 0.05 per cent level

Appendix 4

Crisis perception hypotheses

A Hypotheses from the study by North, et al[1]

1 The higher the tension, the stronger the tendency for élite perceptions of the crisis to coalesce around a few simplified stereotypes and a limited range of alternatives.

2 The higher the tension, the stronger the tendency for rumour to be transmitted as fact.

3 The higher the tension, the narrower the range of perceived alternatives and the more restricted the ability to assess the probable consequences of each possible choice.

4 The higher the tension, the stronger the tendency to make decisions on the basis of effective feelings rather than cognitive calculations.

5 The higher the tension, the stronger is the tendency for a state to perceive another state primarily in terms of whether the state is 'with us or against us'.

6 The higher the tension, the stronger the tendency for state A either to perceive the crisis in terms which enhance its own self-defensive role; or to make choices which reveal its opponent B, as deserving of the punishing activity which A is contemplating. Under rising tension, state B may be expected to behave similarly.

7 If a state's perception of injury to itself is sufficiently great, this perception will offset perceptions of insufficient capability, making the perception of capability much less important a factor in a decision to go to war.

8 The higher the tension, the stronger the tendency to assess the probable rewards of early action high and the danger of punishment low: concomitantly, the tendency will be to estimate the probable rewards of delay as low and the dangers of punishment as high.

9 The higher the tension, the stronger the tendency to assess the rewards of violence as high and the rewards of non-violent action as low.

10 The higher the tension, the less the ability to seek new solutions to a conflict and the stronger the tendency to choose alternatives habitually associated with the kind of crisis which is perceived.

11 The higher the tension, the stronger the tendency to rely on habitual images and stereotypes.

12 The higher the tension, the stronger the tendency to interpret a conciliatory move on the part of an opponent as a trick, or a sign of weakness, or both.

13 The higher the tension, the stronger the tendency to accept suspicions and fears as facts.

B Hypotheses from the study by Pool and Kessler[2]

14 People pay more attention to trusted, liked sources.

15 People pay more attention to information bearing on actions they have already taken, i.e. action increases commitment.

C Hypotheses from the study by Herman[3]

16 In a crisis a nation's decision makers are more likely to take an action response than in non-crisis.

17 In crisis as compared with non-crisis the more hostility a nation's decision-makers perceive the crisis source to have displayed toward their nation, the more likely is action.

18 In crisis the more the decision-makers perceive their national survival to be endangered the more likely is action rather than inaction.

19 In crisis the higher the priority previously assigned by the decision makers to a goal that becomes endangered the more likely is action than inaction.

20 In crisis the larger the quantity of capabilities possessed by a nation experiencing the situation the more likely is action than inaction.

21 In crisis the more effective conflict that exists amongst a nation's decision-makers the less likely is action rather than inaction.

22 In crisis as compared with non-crisis the more extensive the decision makers search for alternative methods of handling the situation the more likely is action.

[1] R. North *et al.*, *Content Analysis: a handbook with applications for the study of international crisis*, North Western University Press, 1963.

[2] I. Pool and A. Kessler, 'The Kaiser, the Czar and the computer. Information processing in a crisis', *American Behavioural Scientist*, 1965, pp. 31–8.

[3] C. Herman, *Crisis in Foreign Policy Making: A Simulation of International Politics*, Princeton University Press, 1965 (duplicated).

Index